INCREASE
YOUR LEARNING POWER

by
GEOFFREY A. DUDLEY
B.A.(Lond.)

*Director of Studies, Psychology House,
Marple, Cheshire*

With an Appendix on
HOW TO READ FASTER

foreword by Melvin Powers

Published by
Melvin Powers
WILSHIRE BOOK COMPANY
12015 Sherman Road
No. Hollywood, California 91605
Telephone: (213) 875-1711

By the same author:
  Dreams, Their Meaning and Significance (American edition:
    How to Understand Your Dreams)
  The Right Way to Interpret Your Dreams
  Self-Help for Self-Mastery
  Your Personality
  Rapid Reading
  Use Your Imagination

Translations:
  Yoga Asanas (by Louis Frédéric)
  About Fasting (by Otto H. F. Buchinger)

Printed by

HAL LEIGHTON PRINTING COMPANY
P.O. Box 3952
North Hollywood, California 91605
Telephone: (213) 983-1105

Printed in the United States of America

ISBN-0-87980-085-2

CONTENTS

PREFACE 7

1 WHAT IS MEMORY? 13

    1. The "Thingummybob" Principle—2. "Faculty" Psychology—3. Different Types of Memory—4. Types of Memory Images—5. Ways of Remembering

2 WHY WE FORGET 23

    1. Weak Impression—2. Disuse—3. Interference—4. Repression—(a) Experimental Proofs of Repression—(b) Memory Optimists and Pessimists—(c) Lack of Early Memories (Infantile Amnesia)—(d) Early Memories—(e) Disturbance of Memory for Recent Events (Senile Amnesia)—(f) Déjà Vu

3 HOW TO REMEMBER 45

    1. Impression—(a) Habit—(b) Interest—(c) Relaxation—(d) Worry or Emotional Conflict—Summary of Advice on How to Concentrate—2. Repetition—(a) The Law of Comprehension (Memory and Meaning)—(b) Spaced Learning ("Little and Often")—(c) The Law of Recitation—(d) The Law of Overlearning—(e) The Law of Whole Learning—(f) The Law of Confidence—(g) Reintegration—(h) Memory for Completed and Uncompleted Tasks (Zeigarnik Effect)—(i) Figure and Ground (von Restorff Effect)—3. Avoiding Interference—4. Repression—(a) The Solution of Problems in Sleep—(b) Free Association—(c) Laws of Association—(d) How to Use Association—(e) How to Remember a Speech

4 HOW TO FORGET 96

    1. *Weak Impression*—2. *Disuse*—3. *Interference*—4. *Repression*

5 SUMMARY OF PRACTICAL HINTS ON REMEMBERING AND
    FORGETTING 102

    1. *What is Memory?*—2. *Why Do We Forget?*—3. *How Can We Remember?*—4. *How Can We Forget?*— *"Refresh Your Memory" Quiz—Key to "Refresh Your Memory" Quiz*

APPENDIX (HOW TO READ FASTER) 114

REFERENCES 120

SOME OTHER BOOKS ON MEMORY 124

INDEX 126

FOREWORD

From time to time, never often enough, a book is published in which all the platitudes concerning the achievement of success have been excluded, and the reader is given a realistic view of the learning process that must precede the attainment of any worthwhile goals.

This is such a book. In it, Geoffrey A. Dudley, a British psychologist, analyzes methods that will increase your ability to learn whatever you may need to learn in your quest for success or even for the sheer joy of learning so that you can understand the many new scientific and cultural facets of our modern civilization.

Mr. Dudley's methods are psychologically sound, and have proved workable in everyday life as well as in the smaller but easier controlled laboratory setting which first indicated statistically that they would be of general help. The techniques differ in some ways from the more euphoric and often falsely optimistic ones offered by many self-improvement books, but they actually offer a quicker change in your life if you will follow them.

This is always the case when tested techniques are contrasted with grandiose "pie-in-the-sky" schemes which are almost utterly divorced from practicality and reality and offer only manufactured proof. The recent history of publishing, however, shows that a large segment of the American public is seeking a formula that will produce success without the effort of learning special skills or, for that matter, even learning how to learn.

It is to the latter point that Mr. Dudley devotes his book. He is convinced that most people do not pursue wildly impractical goals by attempting to use equally impractical methods because of some inherent or acquired flaw in their personality. He believes, rather, that they are ignorant of productive learning processes and I, for one, am prepared to believe him because educational methods in the last few years have changed almost as fast as the weather.

It has become clear to me, in teaching a weekly lecture course, that the bitter feuds and fast changing viewpoints of educators have produced a vast confusion even in individuals who are strongly motivated to learn. That is why almost any road to learning or success which detours around all of the controversial educational methods finds eager believers and practitioners.

I am not going to name the various educational methods which have gained ascendancy for long or short periods of time since John Dewey first instituted the winds of modern change, but any experienced teacher of advanced education can foretell the educational gaps which will predominate in any particular age group. As recently as 1962, I wrote a book, [1] in collaboration with Robert S. Starrett, in which Thomas M. Cooley II, dean of the School of Law, University of Pittsburgh, revealed to the *Saturday Review* that some of his students could not spell well enough to look up words in a dictionary.

It has been my experience that, aside from an inability to spell, many students cannot read with enough speed to cover assigned material, and this problem is compounded by the fact that they do not fully comprehend what they do read because they do not know the rudiments of concentration. This is saddening when one contemplates the marvelous potentialities of the human brain.

Of course, the inability to comprehend advanced material is closely tied to one's failure to remember relevant material which is assumed by most educators to have been mastered at some earlier time, and it is for this reason that Mr. Dudley first discusses memory. It is an intricate and greatly misunderstood faculty, one that requires refreshing from time to time.

One of the first things readers of this book will learn is that there are two major classifications of memory labeled "Immediate" and "Remote." Generations of students who have crammed feverishly for examinations do not have to be told that memory for something that has been read recently

[1] *A Practical Guide to Better Concentration,* Melvin Powers/Robert S. Starrett, Wilshire Book Company, 1962.

is better than for something that has been read in the past, but this is obviously not the whole answer or we would all have to continually study material already stored by our brain cells.

The fact that students cram indicates they know intuitively or by experience that they can retain memory for a few hours easier than a few weeks or months, but this does not explain how, for example, we remember without effort the dates 1492, 1776 and 1812. Mr. Dudley explains how this is possible when he compares *rote* memory with *logical* memory.

By and large, rote memory is employed when there is no other way to learn except by sheer repetition as in the case of multiplication tables. Actually, less repetition is involved when logic is employed, yet it is at the point where this type of learning begins to predominate that the dropout figure begins to rise.

There are many reasons for this, of course, in addition to the new method of learning being used. Economics play a large part in the dropout rate, but other factors are even more important. Many students grow discouraged and quit their studies more or less precisely at the moment when future learning is directly coupled with what they have learned in the past. If they have formed bad learning habits, they can make no further progress and usually develop feelings of inferiority that beset them the rest of their lives.

This indicates, particularly for adults who were late in becoming motivated to learn, that some "unlearning" of inefficient learning habits must take place before a goal-oriented learning process can begin. This is not as difficult as it sounds, for Ivan Pavlov (1849-1936), the great Russian physiologist, performed many experiments both in learning and unlearning that showed unlearning can be accomplished by reversing the former learning process.

It is part of the "Reinforcement" theory of learning, based largely on Pavlov's conditioned reflex, that the best way to eliminate a bad habit is to withhold the reinforcement which occurs each time it is utilized. Unfortunately, it is reinforced even when its utilization leads to further confusion and despair. But proper learning habits can be superimposed over and eventually "neutralize" bad learning patterns.

Although Pavlov's experiments were chiefly on animals, psychologists have found they are almost equally applicable to humans. For example, the environment in which one attemps to learn is an important link in the chain of behavior that affects learning.

If you are accustomed to trying to learn in a room in which there are many potential distractions such as television, radio, popular magazines and other objects which continually have lured you from more vital ways of spending your time, it would be better if you sought more austere surroundings. The artist or writer creating deathless works in a bare garret is not necessarily true—but it is far from being altogether false. Opulence has contributed to the fall of many empires.

There are many other procedures that have been proved helpful to learning. Mr. Dudley mentions it is better to study often for a short time than to study intermittently for a great length of time. It has also been proved that you will remember better if you sleep immediately after learning something rather than continue on to other subjects or new experiences.

Psychologists explain this by stating that a "memory trace" is easily disturbed for the first few minutes after it is formed. Apparently, a memory must be allowed to "set" for a period of time or it will be more difficult to recall.

Obviously, it is not always possible to sleep or rest before going on to other things, but it has also been proved that the first memory trace will be more easily recalled if the second trace is from an unrelated field. Thus students would do better to go from English to mathematics rather than from English to French.

One of the most important points Mr. Dudley makes is that it is *normal* to forget most of what we learn in a few days unless we repeatedly recall it to our conscious mind. It is hoped that this information will reassure legions of persons who believe that they suffer from a congenitally poor memory, and therefore cannot learn anything of a difficult nature.

I think some reliable figures quoted by Mr. Dudley bear repeating here. He cites the case of a prominent psychologist who found that he could not remember 56 percent of the material he had studied one hour later. After nine hours only a further 8 percent had been forgotten, and only 6 percent more had not been retained after two days. In the remainder of a month just 7 percent more had been lost.

These experiments, conducted repeatedly, showed that approximately 70 percent of the memory loss in the month was forgotten in the first hour. Surely this points up the extreme importance of reflecting for an hour or more on all important facts we learn. You might start this sort of learning process by memorizing these figures so that they come easily to mind two days from now.

Many direct mail businesses and television advertisers have learned that bunching a group of letters or commercials closely together is more effective than spacing them out over a long period, thus paying unwitting tribute to a fundamental law of psychology. Carrying this a bit further, don't give those you wish to influence enough time to forget you. Clearly, it would be of benefit to me if you would remember this as Powers' law.

It is axiomatic to say that pleasant memories are recalled more easily than unpleasant ones, but we have to use the psychiatric term "repression" to explain why this happens. And it has to have deeper implications than "My Most Embarrassing Moment" before it occurs.

Repression is evoked to keep ideas from the conscious mind when the ideas are not only unpalatable but completely unacceptable to the individual's image of himself. It might happen, for example, when a devoted Christian reads atheistic material, particularly if it sounds plausible and arouses involuntary doubts.

Even a psychiatrist, in pursuing his learning, may banish

to the unconscious mind certain emotional reactions which he knows, but does not wish to recognize or remember, are part of his behavioral pattern. In all such incidents, however, it must be realized that repression is never desirable. Self-knowledge is one of the important attributes of learning, and one can never gain too much knowledge.

In order to amplify this last statement, you might like to recall the old adage, "A little knowledge is a dangerous thing." The Christian and the psychiatrist could have resolved their conflicts if they had kept them in the conscious mind. It is easier to vanquish a foe who is in the open than one who lurks unseen in the jungle. Psychiatry recognizes the truth of this by trying to unlock the unconscious mind by processes known as abreaction, regression and revivification.

Briefly, we can sum up memory in a negative fashion by stating that we forget because we lack concentration and motivation strong enough to create even the brief impression necessary to ensure the reflection which makes it more lasting. We also forget when we pile one idea on another too rapidly or when the wish not to remember (repression) is stronger than the wish to remember.

One thing is certain. Barring certain physiological problems which I shall mention a little further on, you must resist the desire to explain your inability to learn on your memory. You are equipped with the most awesome apparatus for remembering in the world, far more intricate than the most advanced computer.

At this point, I think it is important to say a little bit about computers inasmuch as many people in certain positions feel they are a threat to their present security. Undoubtedly, in many cases, this is true, but it is also true that computers will allow man to enjoy more interesting occupations than he can now imagine if he is willing and able to learn.

It is imperative to remember that computers, although they can perform functions with an immediacy man can never hope to duplicate, must be programmed to perform those functions by man. An unprogrammed computer is no more than scrap metal.

The argument as to whether a computer can be creative seems academic to me in light of the fact that man must first determine its course of action. So long as man envisions its goals, it cannot properly be thought of as creative even though it may eventually arrive at conclusions that *seem* self-determined.

In speaking of computers, it is impossible not to speak of the vast amount of information about learning contributed by the late Dr. Norbert Wiener, father of Cybernetics and one of the world's most remarkable mathematicians. His contributions are already revolutionizing many fields, including learning.

The fascinating Wiener story began when he introduced methods of improving mechanical systems, but he went from there to prediction machines, improving the results of anti-aircraft fire which could, with information programmed into the gun control itself, pinpoint an airplane travelling rapidly through the air and bring it down. It was a most sophisticated instrument, but here again the extraordinary results depended on statistical data furnished by man.

It soon became apparent to Wiener that the same methods could be applied to man, and Dr. Maxwell Maltz, a plastic surgeon, recognized the clinical applications of his theory in his best selling book, *Psycho-Cybernetics.*[2] By its use, along with Self-Image psychology, many patients attained self-esteem and began to lead productive lives.

The key word to the precision of Dr. Wiener's machines was "feedback," and there is sometimes only a semantic difference between his approach and that of Mr. Dudley. For instance, the immediate reflection of the latter is very similar to the feedback of Wiener which proceeds backward from a poor performance, changing the unsuccessful method and pattern of the poor performance by a process of checks and balances we can call learning.

In machines, such as a missile, positive feedback is re-

[2]*Psycho-Cybernetics*, Maxwell Maltz, M.D., Wilshire Book Company, 1963.

sponsible for keeping it on a collision course with its target, but if it should begin to err, negative feedback will bring it back on course. In its simplest human terms, this latter process might be called learning from our mistakes; that is, we have reflected on our error (feedback) long enough to know when and why they occur, and can make corrections.

Regrettably, in the human system, there comes a time when corrections can no longer be made. The time varies but the symptoms are unmistakable. They follow the onset of the period when our body and mind fall heir to the degenerative diseases.

All of us are familiar with the elderly individual who remembers perfectly the events of his childhood, but cannot remember what happened an hour ago. We say that such persons are in their second childhood, but psychiatrists say they are suffering from senile amnesia.

From this point on, no more learning is possible although gerontologists (physicians who specialize in geriatrics, and are learning how to postpone the degenerative period) are doing a great deal to help this rapidly increasing group. Mr. Dudley names some of the other things that may prematurely cause this condition.

This book contains many seemingly strange manifestations of memory, perhaps the strangest being the phenomenon of *déjà vu,* a term that literally means "already seen." Probably we have all experienced it, and some of us, undoubtedly, have thought we possessed unique psychic powers as a result.

This phenomenon is the feeling that you have previously experienced, in exactly the same way, something that is occurring at the moment. Enough clinical material has accumulated to indicate that this feeling probably results from an earlier and similar or associated experience that has been forgotten. So much for this apparently occult power—at least for the present.

Returning to more practical matters, it is not an overstatement to say that learning uninteresting material is the most difficult of problems. The answer is the usage of techniques employed by Emile Coué, a French psychologist who was very much in vogue here during the 1920's, and whose philosophy still persists.

Millions of Americans of an earlier era repeated Coué's formula, "Every day, in every respect, I am getting better and better," and a variation of this phrase is the best way, according to Mr. Dudley, to learn uninteresting material. He suggests repeating, "This interests me and I'll remember it," and "This work is interesting me more and more." Like all rote learning, this is eventually accepted as true and the fanaticism of Communists or Fascists are frightening examples of its powerful effect.

This repetitive type of learning indicates Emile Coué might have had some influence on England where Mr. Dudley lives, but that isn't important. The fact is that auto-suggestion or repeated suggestions from others are the only things that work when you *must* learn something which is uninteresting at present, but is necessary in attaining future goals or is opposed to human nature.

This learning manual contains many more proved methods of learning that I have attempted to reinforce or supplement in this foreword, but it is time Mr. Dudley had the floor to himself.

In conclusion, I wish you success and good luck in mastering these techniques that can improve your learning power. And by way of a postscript, I might add there are other effective ways to learn after you are sure you can *remember* the ones in this book.

Melvin Powers

12015 Sherman Road
No. Hollywood, California 91605

PREFACE

THIS book is different from other books on learning and memory in several ways. First of all, it does not subscribe to the belief that there is such a thing as memory. A memory is not something that we possess; the word does not correspond to any faculty in the mind. Rather, remembering is something that we do or that the brain does. "Memory" is postulated to account for the fact that we remember. This fact is the only evidence for its existence. This book, therefore, deals directly with what we do, i.e., remember, not indirectly with something, i.e., memory, which is supposed to make that activity possible.

Secondly, this book does not subscribe to the belief that memory can be improved. This is not the same thing as saying that we cannot remember better. We can remember better but it is not because our memory can be improved; it is because we can improve our methods of memorising and recalling. No scientific evidence is so far available which would suggest that there is any way of improving the brain's sheer power of retaining what is memorised. Indeed, there is plenty of evidence that as we grow older this power of retention actually deteriorates.

Thirdly, this is not a book for those who like advice unsupported by scientific evidence. In writing it we have not sat down and indulged in theorising about how we remember. We have gone to those who have actually studied the ways in which people remember, i.e., the psychologists who have conducted laboratory experiments on the subject. And plenty of experiments have been conducted in this field—enough, I believe, to justify making those findings more widely known to the general public. For over fifteen years the author has combed the research literature and textbooks for information on what psychologists have discovered about memory. This book is the result.

If there are any mistakes or shortcomings in it, the author accepts full responsibility and would be grateful to have them pointed out to him. Any credit for the practical value of what is discussed herein, however, should go to others. It belongs to the

7

research psychologists who have conducted careful and painstaking experiments to find out exactly how people remember and what conditions favour their remembering better.

Of course, it would be fallacious to suppose that the last word has been said on this subject. But the author has striven to make the information contained in these chapters as up to date as possible. If he has missed out any important research findings that should have been included, or has failed to draw any practical conclusion that seems justified, he offers his sincere apologies for it.

The purpose of this book, then, is twofold: to acquaint the reader with what psychologists have discovered about learning, remembering and forgetting, and to suggest practical ways of making use of that knowledge.

It contains no magical formula for becoming a mental prodigy. It does not purport to show you how to develop a "photographic memory." It offers no guarantee that with its aid you will win a big prize on a TV quiz show. Nor does it advance any claim to have discovered some occult method of memory training of which psychology is still ignorant. It is written for sensible men and women who recognise that there are limits to what we can or should learn and remember, but who share the author's view that these limits need not be too cramping nor too insurmountable.

Much of our learning is dependent upon the kind of motivation which lies behind our behaviour. By motivation we mean those persistent conditions within ourselves which move us to act.

Some controversy exists about whether these motives are innate or whether they are derived from experience. Psychologists who subscribe to the "innate" view list various instincts as the primary sources of behaviour. Some examples of these instincts are: sex, hunger, curiosity, aggressiveness, etc. Other psychologists believe that the individual learns to act as he does in certain situations as a result of his early childhood training.

At present this controversy cannot be settled to the satisfaction of both schools. For the time being the most reasonable attitude to take is that of supposing that both innate drives and upbringing contribute determinants of our behaviour, including our behaviour in learning situations.

Such a view is consistent with the fact that individuals differ in the degree and range of their motivation. Some students will learn out of love of the subject-matter itself, while others need some ulterior purpose to assist them; they need to be able to find in their learning some practical value or some way of furthering their personal ambitions. The task of the school is to foster both types of motivation and to provide the proper conditions that will encourage both types of learners.

We have spoken so far of motives which are conscious, but psycho-analysis has also accustomed us to think in terms of unconscious motivation. Unconscious motives can both assist and interfere with learning. Probably the latter type of situation is the more common. The type of child who is referred to the Child Guidance Clinic is likely to be the one in whom unconscious motives arising from family problems, insecurity, emotional conflicts, etc., are interfering with the mastery of school subjects. Such children can be greatly helped by being encouraged to "work off" their repressed feelings in various ways, e.g. finger painting, play therapy, etc. When this has been done the child can return to the school and make normal progress in his or her studies.

We see, then, that motivation exerts an important influence upon success and failure in studies. It can, without doubt, make a vast difference to the amount learned and how well it is learned. In whatever we try to learn, therefore, we should make an effort to link it to some motive which is prominent in our lives. If you are studying something which you don't see the need of, try to find in it some advantage which will give you a motive for doing your best at it. The good teacher is the one who can help his pupils to tie up the school subjects with their motives in this way.

The author's main debt is to the psychologists who have undertaken the research upon which this book relies heavily. I am grateful for the privilege of drawing upon the studies which are cited in these pages. I hope that those responsible for them will feel that the debt has been repaid if this book succeeds in making their findings known to a wider section of the public.

The cases cited in the text have been drawn from the author's twenty years' experience as a psychological consultant. The author must express his deep appreciation and gratitude to those persons upon whose experiences he has drawn in this way. He would not have presumed to offer his advice to others had not those who have used it proved its value for themselves.

The author can ask no better reward than that the reader may be encouraged to use the practical hints which others have used, and by reading these pages may achieve a better understanding of the functions of remembering and forgetting.

"Memory," says Dr. Erwin Dunlop, "is like Janus, the god of the new year. It faces backward to the past, relates the past to the present, and from this basis it determines our future. We are what we are, because we remember. Memory is the instrument that preserves the continuity of our experience, and thus shapes our whole personality." (1)*

GEOFFREY A. DUDLEY

Cheadle,
Cheshire.

* For references see page 120.

TO EVA, MUM, DAD, JOAN,
SUSAN AND CAROL

ACKNOWLEDGMENTS

I WOULD like to express my gratitude to Margaret Fryer, who typed the manuscript with her usual painstaking and cheerful efficiency.

CHAPTER I

WHAT IS MEMORY?

1. THE "THINGUMMYBOB" PRINCIPLE

As you read the opening words of this chapter, an image of what you read is being formed in your mind. In fact, all the things you experience with your senses are stored as mental images. These mental images can be revived because *every experience that we undergo is recorded in the brain and nervous system.* That is why we are able to remember our experiences.

This basic fact of mental life, upon which both remembering and forgetting depend, was called by the American psychologist William James the *"thingummybob" principle.*

Remembering, then, means *attending to a mental image which has been determined by a past experience.* It is the power to retain knowledge in the mind, to recall impressions of past events. The past is brought into the present by means of mental images of the things perceived by the sense organs.

The ideas of memory may originate in actual experiences or in ideas of such experiences. That is to say, I can remember an experience and I can also remember having remembered it.

In actual practice a group of similar experiences is revived as often as a single past experience. For example, when we remember what a bicycle looks like, we may not remember a particular bicycle. Rather we have a memory image compounded of the memory images of many bicycles which we have seen.

If, as we have said, remembering depends upon images, how does it differ from imagination and thinking? Images play a part in these mental activities too. The difference is one of function, not of the material of which the images are composed. The function of images in memory is to represent past experiences. In imagination the images relate to what is thought of as occurring in the future.

Past experience, too, is made use of in thinking. Whereas remembering is a direct use of what has been learned, thinking is an indirect use. Remembering is repeating something previously experienced, while thinking is doing something partly original.

What makes it possible for us to remember at all? The answer to this question has to be sought in the brain. Two theories of how the mental image is stored in the brain hold the field. One is that it lays down an actual physical impression in the brain structure called a memory trace. The other and more recent view is that memories are stored in the form of patterns of electrical impulses which have no fixed location in any particular area of the brain.

There is evidence in support of both views and at present it is impossible to decide between them. It may even be that both views are true and that there are memories of two types: those laid down in a particular area of the brain and those existing as patterns of electrical stimulation.

2. "Faculty" Psychology

Whatever the truth, one thing is clear. There is no such thing as "the memory." People often complain: "I find great difficulty in remembering what I read. I want you to tell me how to train the memory." One can understand the need that prompts such a request, but psychologists are not very fond of referring to *the* memory.

There are several reasons for this. One is that to speak of the memory suggests that it is a thing. It creates a picture of there being in the head a little box into which we pop our memories and from which they pop out again. This is, of course, not true.

Secondly, it suggests that if there were such a thing as the memory we should have only one of it. This, too, is not true. The truth is that we have different memories for different kinds of material. In the same person some of these memories may be good and others not so good. For example, a man said: "I have an excellent memory for names and faces, but I find it difficult to memorise facts connected with my professional accountancy studies."

Another man said: "My memory for knowledge directly connected with my job and my hobby is very good. The names of people, however, are an entirely different matter and most of the time I cannot remember them."

Thirdly, memory is not really something static. It is a dynamic process or mental activity; it is something that a person does, not something that he possesses. It would be better to say that he remembers than that he has a memory or memories.

The idea of there being a memory, however, is so firmly rooted that we will use it for the sake of convenience. As we do it should be borne in mind that we are thinking of the activity of remembering, not of the possession of a faculty of memory.

To speak of the memory harks back to a past tradition in psychology, when it was fashionable to believe in what are known as mental faculties. "Faculty" psychology, which sponsored this view, taught that there exists a number of discrete mental faculties, each of which is responsible for all mental acts of a particular kind. For example, all acts of remembering were held to be due to the existence of a faculty of memory; all acts of willing to a faculty of will. Other "faculties" were reason, imagination, perception, judgment, etc.

This view belongs to the era when psychology was called "mental philosophy"—an old-fashioned term no longer in use. Once very popular, faculty psychology is now discredited. The evidence against it is provided by such observations as that in ageing people a very poor memory for recent events may coexist with an excellent one for events of the distant past. Obviously, then, there cannot be a general faculty of memory which is responsible for both kinds of remembering.

The point that memory is not a single faculty may be illustrated from the life of a certain professor of medicine. We are told that as a young man he had such a remarkable memory that he could glance over a page of Shakespeare selected at random and then repeat it word for word. Yet it was not unusual for him to forget to put on his collar and tie or jacket when he left home to lecture to his students.

In this case an excellent memory for Shakespeare coexisted with a very poor memory for the ordinary details of life. The professor was, in fact, absent-minded only for certain things. This he could not have been if all his memory activities had been governed by the work of a single "faculty."

A person may acquire marvellous memory power for knowledge gained along a certain line and yet be hopelessly inadequate in recalling items unconnected with his particular interest. Someone may readily memorise and recall facts, but have little success in remembering figures and dates. Another person may remember faces more easily than he can recall tones of voice. One may keep in mind events of history, both ancient and modern, but be unable to recite biographical details.

These illustrations show that there is no unitary "faculty" of memory. "The 'faculty' of memory," writes Dr. A. A. Roback, a modern psychologist, "would denote that somewhere in the mind there is a force or power which enables us to remember, no matter what the material, whether figures, objects, meaningless words, or significant ideas."

Questioning whether an understanding of the mind can be based on the view that it is composed of faculties, Dr. Roback concludes: "The chief argument against faculty psychology was that it explained nothing; that it was, therefore, a sterile attempt to give information which was of no value." (2)

3. DIFFERENT TYPES OF MEMORY

There are two main types of remembering activity. The first is that involved in such apparently simple tasks as writing and speaking, which it would be impossible to carry out unless we had learned and remembered them in childhood. On the other hand, there is the remembering activity involved in attending to a present experience which is determined by a particular past experience, as, for example, when we remember now where we spent our last summer holidays.

The first type of memory is called *habit memory*; the second type is called *pure memory*. When we speak of memory we may mean either or both of these types, although we generally mean the second. In this book we shall be chiefly concerned with pure memory.

Habit memory is the knowledge acquired by experience as distinct from the particular experience of acquiring it. When we have learned to play a piece of music, we are said to remember it, but we may not remember the particular experiences of learning it. Playing a musical composition, which is remembered in the sense of being learned by heart, has all the marks of a habit. Like a habit it is acquired by repetition.

Pure memory, on the other hand, is the activity of attending to a particular experience, as, for example, when I remember what I ate for my Christmas dinner last year.

The past, then, survives under two distinct forms: first, in motor mechanisms (habit); secondly, in independent recollections (pure memory).

Remembering activities are also capable of being classified in various other ways. For instance, there are *immediate memory* and *remote memory*.

When we attempt to reproduce what we have learned, we can do so at once, in which case we are testing immediate memory. For example, when you use the index of a book, you need to remember the page number only long enough to find the reference you want.

One of the simplest memory experiments measures the immediate memory span. A set of letters or a row of numbers is presented, and you are required to reproduce as many as you can remember after seeing or hearing them once only. For example, look at the set of letters on the left below:

P   X   M
S   C   L   729438651
Z   N   G

Now close the book and try to write down what you saw. Afterwards do the same with the row of numbers.

Few people are able to reproduce more than seven or eight letters or digits correctly. The average immediate memory span for digits is about seven.

Immediate memory is contrasted with remote memory. This is tested when we try to recall something after a lapse of time. If after we have learned a certain lesson we reproduce what we have learned before we have had time to forget any appreciable amount, we speak of immediate memory. If we delay the occasion on which we reproduce the learned material until some time after having learned it, we can then use remote memory.

In addition, memory can be classified on the basis of the method used in memorising. When we memorise by repetition alone, we are using *rote memory*. On the other hand, when we try to fit the parts into a unified whole, we employ *logical memory*. Usually fewer repetitions are necessary for fixing the facts in mind when the logical method is employed.

The child who learns the multiplication tables is said to employ rote memory, while the adult who learns by observing relationships is said to employ logical memory. Children later begin to learn by logical memorising, but even the adult does not scorn rote memory at times. This is because the material that he has to learn is not always full of meaning. Such material can, however, often be remembered quite well, especially if a person is interested in it. When we are dealing with material which cannot easily be organised into a meaningful whole, this is where rote memory, which depends purely and simply upon repetition, comes in handy.

For instance, when we are learning words in a foreign language, the form of the word may not have much meaning for us. It may seem to be just a peculiar jumble of syllables that we cannot readily associate with either the English equivalent or any other English word. It is then that we must rely upon rote memory.

4. Types of Memory Images

Most memory images are inferior in realism to actual sensory experience. That is to say, remembering something is never as vivid as seeing it. But individuals differ greatly in the realism of their memory images.

For example, some children under fourteen, if they examine any picture closely for a few moments and then look at a plain grey background, can see the object as if it were present. They can answer questions about it which they did not have in mind while looking at it. This type of image is called an *eidetic image*. Eidetic imagery seems to fade out during adolescence. Although a few adults can still obtain eidetic images, most are incapable of doing so.

Another type of memory experience which shows considerable individual differences is the *hallucination*. An hallucination is a memory image which seems real, until you awaken to the reality of your surroundings, or because you have lost contact with the objective situation, e.g. in dreams, mental illness. It is built up out of past experience and taken for a present objective fact.

When we see "something tha ' 't there," the hallucination is fabricated out of something already in our mind. Something cannot be created out of nothing in the mental realm any more than it can in the physical realm.

For example, on entering a psycho-analyst's consulting-room a patient thought that he saw a pool of blood in a corner and that the analyst had been murdered by the previous patient. In the course of the analytic session it turned out that it was the patient himself who felt murderous towards the analyst. In projecting the memories of his murderous wishes on to the previous patient, he became convinced that the latter had murdered the analyst. (3)

This incident illustrates how the projection of a memory image leads to the development of an hallucination. The patient "saw" the blood which wasn't there because he had a reason for doing so. The hallucination was created out of memories that already existed in his own mind.

Such experiences can be produced in the psychological laboratory. One psychologist sat his subjects in a chair, on the arm of which was a small light-bulb. He then sounded a thousand-cycle tone, and at the same time the bulb was lit up. The tone and the light were paired for sixty trials. Eventually thirty-two of forty subjects reported hearing the tone when the light was presented alone.

Four other psychologists were run through the procedure. Two of them were conditioned into hearing the tone as an auditory hallucination. (4)

There are also differences from one person to another regarding the type of imagery they employ in remembering. This naturally leads to distinctive preferences for material presented in a certain way.

For example, the following report illustrates a preference for "learning by doing": "I understand by being shown how to do a job and having it explained as I progress, but I am never able to understand much how to do a job by reading about it in a book and following diagrams, etc."

This person evidently remembers best by means of images of the muscular movements made in carrying out a piece of work. There are also memory images of the senses of sight, hearing, touch, taste and smell.

Many people are visiles, that is to say, they remember better by creating visual images of what they learn. A preference for a visual presentation is revealed in the following report: "I have to draw a diagram to illustrate the process of thought before I have got it permanently. Otherwise I waste hours memorising the results."

This lady's report may be contrasted with the one given above. Another point worth noting is that she is using the word "memorising" in a restricted sense. She refers to memorising verbal material, such as the words printed in a book. When she draws a diagram, however, she is also memorising. She is making use of visual memory; that is to say, she finds it more convenient to learn pictorial than verbal material.

On the other hand, another person said that he found it easier to concentrate on material treated orally, i.e. talks or lectures. Such a person is of an imagery type known as an audile. This type can remember better by hearing the spoken word than by seeing the printed word.

A few people are tactiles; that is, they can remember things better when they have felt them. Their remembering is based on images of touch. For example, a woman said: "My memory of touch is far stronger than that of sight. For example, in my mind I can feel a dog's coat, put on its collar, feel it pull at the lead and jump up, sense the warmth of its pads. Or again, I can imagine the vibration of a mechanical digger. But if, for example, I try to remember whether the dog is black or brown, the visual image is vague and soon fades out."

Here is an interesting example of an olfactory memory, i.e., one based on images of the sense of smell. "It is quite surprising how many forgotten things come back to mind," said Mrs. H. W. "Even the smell associated with events of long ago is as real as if I were actually smelling it now."

Individual differences of this kind exist from person to person, and an attempt has been made to classify individuals into types according to the kinds of images which control their remembering. It has been found, however, that in the great majority of cases this classification does not work out very well in practice. It is doubtful whether a particular person belongs to any one of the above types exclusively, for the majority of people employ both visual and auditory images.

In the words of one psychologist, "Instead of a few types, there is one type." This means that most people belong to a mixed type. That is to say, they remember in several different ways, although perhaps one way may predominate, as in the instances cited above.

Hence, it is really up to each person to find the right sort of conditions under which he can memorise most effectively. He may find that it suits him better to say something over aloud a few times to himself, while another person will find it easier to remember by creating a picture in his mind's eye.

5. Ways of Remembering

Remembering, as we see, is not a simple but a complex act. A study of the process permits us to distinguish three separate aspects. In other words, when we remember there are three ways in which we do so.

We can study something to commit it to memory. For example, we can repeat a poem to learn it by heart. This is called *memorising*.

Secondly, we can try to bring to mind something we have temporarily forgotten. For example, we memorised a friend's telephone number yesterday and to-day we try to think what it was. When the attempt is successful, this memory activity is known as *recalling*.

We have seen what must happen to an item between memorising it and recalling it. Obviously, it must somehow be recorded in the brain, otherwise we should be unable to recall it at all. The image was impressed on the mind and some trace of the impression remains. If nothing of it remained, nothing could be revived. The memory activity which keeps, say, the date of the Battle of Hastings in our heads, even though we are not consciously thinking of it, is called *retaining* or *retention*.

There are, then, three ways in which we remember. We memorise, we retain and we recall. Memory depends upon (1) the acquirement of the idea or image to be recalled; (2) the ability to retain the impression which has been made; and (3) the ability to revive or recognise the impression which has been retained. Remembering is to be reduced essentially to these three functions.

The practical question with everyone who would strengthen his memory and make it serviceable and reliable is how to get an idea into the mind so as to get it out again on demand. From a practical point of view the most important of the three functions are the first and third: the acquirement of an idea or image and the recall of that idea or image to consciousness. This furnishes the key to a scientific training of the memory.

CHAPTER 2

WHY WE FORGET

WE have seen that the things we experience form mental pictures which are impressed on our brain as memory traces. Each trace is accompanied by a certain amount of mental energy, which is drawn from other memory traces already laid down. The reason for this is that a person has just so much mental energy to invest in the experiences he undergoes.

When a memory trace had little energy to begin with or has lost it to other memory traces, the experience it represents is said to be forgotten. The trace may not be charged with much initial energy because the experience did not make much of an impression in the first place. On the other hand, the energy it had originally may have been drained off in the formation of new memory traces. The learning of something new usually means that something old has to be unlearned.

A trace which has lost its energy can be recharged by repeating the experience which originally laid it down. This is known as refreshing one's memory. For example, when one forgets a telephone number one can recharge the memory trace by looking the number up in the telephone book.

A poor memory is caused, then, by the memory trace not having much energy to begin with, by not being recharged or fading with the lapse of time, and by losing its energy to other memory traces. That is to say, the causes of forgetting may be grouped under the following headings:

1. Weak impression.
2. Disuse.
3. Interference.

There is also a form of forgetting, known as repression, caused by resistance or opposition from something else in the mind to the recall of the desired memory. We may, therefore, add the following heading:

4. Repression.

Let us consider each of these headings in further detail.

1. WEAK IMPRESSION

The first cause of forgetting is not properly attending to what we wish to remember. The result is that the experience does not make a strong enough impression on us.

Attention means directing mental activity towards a mental or physical object or situation. For example, when I think of something I did last week, I am attending to my memory of the event. This memory is a mental object. On the other hand, when I admire a beautiful view, I am attending to a physical object.

Attention is to the mind what the power of focusing the lens is to a camera. If the camera is not properly focused, the resulting photograph will not be clear. So a wobbly, vagrant mind does not get clear pictures of the things it observes, and consequently finds it difficult to bring them back to memory.

Upon the clearness and truth of first impressions must depend the ease and speed of their reproduction. We cannot hope to recall past events or experiences with certainty if our perception of them is not clear and reliable.

A young man said: "I have a poor memory for names of people, books and places. This failing is worse when I am in the company of important and influential people."

This problem illustrates the effect of inattention upon memory. When he is in the company of influential people, he is probably thinking of the impression which he is making upon them. When their names are announced or when some book or place is mentioned, he probably does not remember it because he is not really attending to it.

The law of attention is that we cannot attend to two separate things at the same time. For example, we cannot simultaneously entertain two opposite thoughts, like "I am a success" and "I am a failure." This law is called by Dr. Henry Knight Miller in his book *Practical Psychology* the law of predominant mental impression. (5)

Although many people try to attend to more than one thing at once, they succeed only in alternating their attention. The attention of the person who is apparently capable of, say, reading a book while he listens to the radio really shifts backwards and forwards in quick succession from one to the other.

The practical use of the law of attention is seen when we realise that it is the first step in all the higher mental processes. The art of memory is primarily the art of attention. We forget because we do not pay sufficient attention to what we wish to remember in order to imprint it firmly on the mind. A good memery, therefore, depends upon attention to what is to be remembered. Since one cannot attend to more than one thing at once, *give your full attention to what you wish to remember*.

2. DISUSE

The second cause of a faulty memory is letting the trace fall into disuse, or not repeating the experience in order to refresh the memory.

It is normal to forget most of what is learned within a few days after learning it—unless it is constantly revised to keep it fresh in mind. For example, a man said: "Whenever I read a book I grasp with ease what it contains, but unfortunately after only a few days I forget almost all of it. What can I do about this?"

A memory trace tends to decay with the lapse of time. For example, another man admitted: "I have a shocking memory. Whatever I study in the morning is forgotten by evening."

Much of what we learn is forgotten almost as soon as we have learned it. The little that remains after that is forgotten more slowly. The psychologist Ebbinghaus, who carried out the most important early work on memory, found that after one hour 56 per cent of the material which he had studied was forgotten; but after nine hours only a further 8 per cent had been forgotten; after two days only a further 6 per cent, and only a further 7 per cent after as long as one month. In other words, about 70 per cent of the amount which was forgotten in the first month was forgotten in the first hour of that month. Consequently, it is most economical to refresh our memory about something as soon as possible afterwards, rather than to wait until some time has elapsed. (6)

This principle is important not only in learning but in teaching, especially in such forms of "teaching" as propaganda, direct-mail advertising, etc. In other words, if a person reads a sales letter, he will forget most of it quite soon afterwards. The rate of forgetting, which is rapid in the first few hours, becomes less rapid later on.

Therefore, how are we to plan a direct-mail advertising campaign in which we are sending out to potential customers a series of, say, six letters about our product? Are we to send one a week for six weeks, or ought we to bunch them together at the start? The above principle suggests that the second method would be the more effective, because if further letters follow immediately after the first one they will have the effect of reinforcing it before the potential customer has forgotten too much of its message.

Although Ebbinghaus worked with nonsense syllables, the same general principle also applies to relatively meaningful material, like follow-up letters, except that meaningful material is as a rule better retained in the memory than meaningless material. It is still true, however, that the rate at which meaningful material is forgotten is also most rapid immediately after it has been studied and less rapid later on.

Experimenting with the same problem, psychologist A. R. Gilliland of Northwestern University found a slower falling off in the rate of initial forgetting in the case of pictures. He showed his subjects pictures, about which he later asked them questions. They were tested immediately after seeing the pictures, and two days, seven days, and thirty days later. One group after two days recalled over four-fifths of what they recalled immediately after seeing the pictures. This points to the effectiveness of suitably chosen visual material in learning, teaching, presenting a sales message, and so on. (7)

A second follow-up reminder is more effective if it is sent out very soon after the first one, but unless it is sent then, it does not matter much whether it is sent ten or thirty days later. The reason is that far more of the message will be forgotten in the first day after the letter is read than between the second and thirtieth days after. The receipt of the second letter should arrest the process of forgetting which began immediately after the prospect had read the first. It refreshes his memory before he has forgotten too much.

That advertisers are aware of the importance of following up soon afterwards may readily be noticed in the course of an evening's TV viewing. It is not at all uncommon to see that the same product is advertised two or three times in the course of the same evening.

3. INTERFERENCE

The above view, however, is too simple. It is now known that other activities we pursue after learning something interfere with our ability to remember it.

We have seen that the material which is newly learned forms a memory trace somewhere in the brain. This is like a plastic material which takes some time to set or consolidate, after which it becomes a part of our store of memories.

However, during the process of hardening or consolidation the memory trace is still susceptible to interference from other mental activities. Psychologists call it "retroactive inhibition." We forget something because of what we do and think afterwards.

"I can wake in the night," said Mr. R. E., "and go over a dream methodically from beginning to end, trying to memorise it. But in the morning it escapes me. I don't know why."

This is an example of retroactive inhibition. It is likely that after he had gone to sleep again, he had further dreams. These caused him to forget the dream which he had committed to memory during the period of wakefulness.

There is a second way in which interference occurs. Work which *precedes* learning also tends to interfere with the retention of the learned material. What happened before an experience causes us to forget it as well as what happened afterwards. This is known as "proactive inhibition."

As we saw in the first chapter, in learning something new there is unlearning of something old. The story is told of a man who was an authority on fishes. He liked to be able to call everybody he met by name. It is said, however, that every time he learned the name of a person he forgot the name of a fish.

4. REPRESSION

There is also a method of unconscious forgetting of painful memories known as "repression." Repression is "the keeping of unacceptable ideas from consciousness, i.e., in the 'unconscious.'" (8) It is the unconscious process whereby we prevent ourselves from becoming aware of some tendency active in the mind. It occurs when two forces in the mind are opposed to each other, the desire to recall being countered by a strong resistance or wish not to recall.

For example, when Berlioz, the famous French composer, was poverty-stricken and his wife was ill, there came to him one night the inspiration for a symphony. He rose from bed, beginning to write, but in his own words he thought: "If I began this bit, I shall have to write the whole symphony. It will be a big thing, and I shall have to spend three or four months over it. That means I shall write no more articles and earn no more money . . . The poor invalid will lack necessities, and I shall be able to pay neither my personal expenses nor my son's fees when he goes on board ship. These thoughts made me shudder, and I threw down my pen, saying, 'Bah, to-morrow I shall have forgotten the symphony.' But the next night I heard the allegro clearly and seemed to see it written down . . . I was going to get up, but the reflections of the day before restrained me. I steeled myself against the temptation and clung to the thoughts of forgetting it. At last I went to sleep, and the next day upon wakening all remembrance of it had indeed gone for ever." Berlioz had, in fact, repressed the memory of the symphony.

Freud has compared repression with what might have happened to a book containing objectionable statements at a time when books were written out by hand. The offending passages would be heavily crossed out, so that when the book was transcribed, gaps in the text would make the passages unintelligible. Or words would be replaced by others and whole new sentences interpolated. Without pressing the analogy too closely, we may say that repression of memories is like the corruption of the text of a book.

Why are memories repressed? It is for two reasons. If a person were to become aware of what is repressed, it would make him anxious and upset him. We more easily forget a memory which conflicts with our comfort or self-esteem than one which does not. This is the law of forgetting by repression.

For example, a man said: "Very occasionally I experience a dream. Then it is usually a horrible one and I forget it as fast as I can. Later I cannot recall even the broadest outline of it." He unconsciously prevented himself from remembering the dream, because the memory made him feel uncomfortable or clashed with his self-esteem.

The second reason is that, although what is repressed may not be unpleasant in itself, it is forgotten because it is associated with something else which is unpleasant. For example, it is easier to forget an appointment to visit the dentist than it is to forget a date to go dancing with a pretty girl. Another instance of unconsciously intentional forgetting due to an experience being associated with something unpleasant is provided by the report of a young man who said: "When attending dancing lessons I feel so foolish and am always successful in forgetting completely any date made for future private lessons, though usually I do not have a forgetful mind."

(a) *Experimental Proofs of Repression*

The occurrence of repression has been demonstrated in the psychological laboratory by means of the following experiment which shows that pleasant experiences are recalled more easily than unpleasant ones.

On returning from the Christmas vacation, a group of college students were asked to record their memories of the vacation. Each memory was then assessed as pleasant or unpleasant. Six weeks later, when the students were retested, the pleasant memories were remembered better than the unpleasant ones. Fifty-three per cent of the pleasant memories were recalled as against only 40 per cent of the unpleasant ones. (9)

A psychologist gave his subjects a list of nouns, to which he asked them to reply with adjectives. Whenever they replied with the name of a colour, they received a mild electric shock. After a while some of them not only stopped naming colours, but apparently failed to think of colours at all. The colour adjectives had been repressed because they had painful associations. (10)

A similar experiment which demonstrates the existence of this mental process is as follows. A list of words was presented to subjects who were asked to give their associations to each one. In the list the word "red" was followed by the word "barn" six times, and whenever this occurred the subject received an unexpected electric shock. The experimenter found that the word which had been followed by the electric shock was forgotten by half of his subjects. (11)

Other experimental proofs of forgetting by repression have been reviewed by Blum and by Zeller. (12, 13)

According to the psycho-analysts, repression is responsible for maladjustment and emotional ill health. We ought, then, to find that the more a person accepts himself the better adjusted he should be. Conversely, the less a person accepts himself the less well adjusted he should be.

This proposition has been validated by the experimental findings of Taylor and Combs. They compared two similar groups of children. One group was composed of better-adjusted children, as assessed by a personality test; the other group of less well-adjusted children, as assessed by the same test.

The psychologists then compiled a list of twenty statements which they regarded as probably true of all children, yet unflattering if admitted to be true, e.g. "I sometimes disobey my parents," "I sometimes tell lies," "I sometimes steal things when I know I will not be caught." The list was presented to both groups of children, and each child was asked to check those statements which were true for him.

The results of the experiment corroborated the psychologists' expectation. They demonstrated that the better adjusted a person is, the better he is able to accept damaging statements about himself. The less well adjusted he is, the greater his resistance against accepting such statements. This experiment confirms the psycho-analytical finding about the connection between maladjustment and the repression of unpleasant truths about oneself. (14)

(b) *Memory Optimists and Pessimists*

Most people, then, remember pleasant experiences better than unpleasant ones. They are known as "memory optimists." For example, a woman may remember the pleasure of holding her baby for the first time better than she remembers the pains of childbirth. Again, Thomas Hood wrote:

> "I remember, I remember, the house where
>   I was born,
>   The little window where the sun came
>   peeping in each morn."

He remembered his birthplace because he found it pleasant to do so. The poet's childhood days were the happiest that he knew.

Another example is that of Mr. I. R., who said: "I have been unsuccessful in trying to recall the name of a person whom I disliked intensely when I knew him fifteen years ago."

One might object, however, that after fifteen years the name might have been forgotten even if he had been emotionally neutral to the man or had liked him. This is true. The above experience, in fact, also illustrates another law of memory.

This is the law of recency, which states that the more recent an experience the better it is remembered. Conversely, the less recent an experience the less well it is remembered. The above name was forgotten not only because it was associated with an unpleasant memory, but also because it was fifteen years ago since it was first learned.

This leads to the question: But there are some things which we remember very well even though they happened long ago; why is this? For example, elderly people can often recall clearly events from their childhood, while they may have forgotten what they were doing ten minutes ago.

This is a special case of forgetting due not to psychological causes but to physical ones. These people are undergoing brain changes with age which impair the retention of recent material. The changes do not, however, disturb the more firmly embedded remote memories of childhood.

The fact that not all people remember pleasant experiences better than unpleasant ones is illustrated by the following reports of persons who may be classed as "memory pessimists."

For example, a young man said: "The memories I recall best are always the same unhappy ones over and over again. I feel that I cannot relax enough to allow my mind to accept any other than these morbid thoughts."

"When I think back," said a young woman, "the only things that spring to mind are my failures and moments of embarrassment."

Another lady, Mrs. H. F., reported: "Generally speaking, I find it less difficult to recall the names of people with whom I have had unhappy associations, even when I have not seen or heard of them for fifteen or twenty years." Her experience, too, illustrates that an unpleasant emotion may contribute to imprinting a memory on the mind so well that it can be recalled after a considerable lapse of time.

Thompson and Witryol investigated the types of unpleasant experiences which adults recall most frequently. Three groups of fifty adults were asked to recall for twenty minutes unpleasant experiences from three periods of childhood and adolescence. From the first five years of life they recalled more physically unpleasant experiences. From the ages of six to twelve years they recalled more unpleasant experiences related to learning to live in a social world. From the ages of twelve to eighteen they recalled more unpleasant experiences generating feelings of inadequacy and insecurity. (15)

Suppose that a woman were to claim that she remembers the pain of childbirth better than the pleasure of holding her baby for the first time. In such a case we might find that the woman had not really wanted a child at all. Holding the baby in her arms for the first time may have been experienced as unpleasant. It may even have been more unpleasant than the pains of childbirth. The woman, therefore, chose to remember the less unpleasant of the two experiences. The less painful memory was more pleasant to her than the more painful one.

The fact seems to be, however, that emotionally charged experiences, whether pleasant or unpleasant, are remembered better than those experiences which are emotionally neutral. At present this point cannot be definitely established. Yet we may say that if two experiences can be recalled equally well and if one is pleasant and the other unpleasant, most of us would probably prefer to remember the pleasant one.

Therefore, we should try to associate what we learn with something pleasant. For example, the name of an hotel can be remembered by associating it with the pleasant holiday we spent there. If we have difficulty in learning a subject, we can use our imagination to picture what it will mean to us to master the material which we are studying. Then we shall experience a feeling of satisfaction which will help us to remember it better.

The causes of forgetting may now be briefly summarised as follows.

1. We forget an experience because it makes a weak impression on us unless we attend to it properly.
2. We forget an experience because we don't refresh our memory of it.
3. We forget an experience because other experiences interfere with it.
4. We forget an experience because it creates a conflict between the wish to remember it and the wish not to remember it.

(c) Lack of Early Memories (Infantile Amnesia)

Before turning to the practical application of the above principles, we may refer to three special problems which forgetting raises. The first is the problem, which everyone encounters, of what Freud calls "the failure of memory for the first years of our lives." The second, which we have briefly touched upon in the previous section, is the loss of memory in ageing persons. The third is the feeling that we sometimes get of "remembering" having seen or done something before when we know that we cannot have seen or done it.

Freud was the first to draw scientific attention to the problem of the lack of memories for the earliest period of our lives. He refers to "the peculiar amnesia which veils from most people (not from all) the first years of their childhood, usually the first six or eight years."

Why cannot we remember what happened to us in our early infancy?

There are several reasons (16):

(1) *Lack of development of mnemonic capacities.* The areas of the brain involved in conscious memory are not fully developed in early infancy.

(2) *Lack of consciousness of self.* In early infancy we have not yet developed the idea that we are individuals, and consequently we do not remember the events of this period as happening to *us*.

(3) *Inability of the infant to verbalise.* We rely on words with which to form memories, and in early infancy we have not yet learned any words. Most adult thinking is done with words or at least with images of things that have names. Before the age of three a person does not know many words or the names of many things. So all that can come to mind is an unnamed feeling about

some unnamed thing. When people have such feelings and don't know where they come from, they may refer to this period preceding the use of words.

(4) *Inability to conceptualise time.* The idea of remembering anything at all implies the ability to distinguish between past and present. The infant has not yet learned how to do this.

(5) *Repression.* Those experiences of early life that we do retain in the form of fantasies have been repressed from conscious memory because they conflict with the demands of reality. According to the doctrine of infantile amnesia propounded by Freud, the experiences of the first six to eight years are cloaked by a curtain of repression.

We have already encountered all but one of these reasons in our discussion of the causes of forgetting in general. The second, third and fourth reasons all come under the heading of "weak impression." The infant's lack of consciousness of self and his inability to use words and conceptualise time mean that his experiences do not impress him strongly enough to be recalled later. The fifth reason, too, applies perhaps more to childhood forgetting than to adult forgetting, since it is in childhood that the basic repressions determining our character are laid down. The first reason is a special physiological one that applies only to childhood.

We see, then, that infantile amnesia is really no more than a special case of the general problem of forgetting. The causes of forgetting in general also account for the particular kind of forgetting that marks the period of infancy.

Nevertheless, the period of infantile amnesia is often interrupted by isolated fragmentary memories. For example, Mr. D. B. said: "Sometimes when I am lying in bed half-way between being awake and asleep my limbs feel short and plump, and the perspective of everything is as if viewed through a wide-angle lens. I always see the same room. One morning I realised that I was feeling as a young baby must in its first twelve months. Could this, in fact, be a memory from my early childhood?"

Such memories are known as "screen memories." If these particular ones are recalled from a period in which most of our experiences have been forgotten, it must be that they are recalled for a special reason.

(d) *Early Memories*

For example, at the age of about sixty, Goethe, in writing an account of his life, recalled a childhood memory of slinging pieces of crockery out of the window into the street, so that they were smashed to pieces. Freud interprets this memory in relation to the fact that a younger brother was born when Goethe was three. The throwing out of the crockery he recognises as a symbolic act of getting rid of the troublesome intruder. Freud considers that Goethe recalled this memory in order to remind himself that he eventually succeeded in preventing the second son from disturbing Goethe's close relation with his mother, for the younger child died when Goethe was nine. (17)

One school of thought believes that these screen memories of early childhood have survived because they embody in a crystallised form the individual's general attitude or "style of life."

For example, Mr. N. S. said: "I recall how in my childhood I was once forced to disclose what had been till then my greatest secret. As an African, I did not get the chance to go to school until I was twelve. I spent most of my time alone as a shepherd boy. As I grew up, I developed an intense curiosity about how everything came into being. 'Why was I born?' I kept on asking myself. In my childish and uneducated way I developed the fantasy that I was born so that the sunlight could strike me before it spread to others. This was to be my 'secret.' One day, when another boy annoyed me, I retaliated by threatening to withhold the sunlight from him. This provoked such laughter that I could not help asking him why he had laughed at me. His reply shattered my illusion and gave me a shock which determined my general attitude to others from that day. I decided that all men are the same and that secrets are useless."

Another example is that of Miss S. A., who said: "I seem to remember posing for a photograph at the front window in my mother's arms. When shown this photo as a schoolgirl I announced that I could remember its being taken, but was laughed down. Two of my brothers are in it, my mother is holding one of my bare feet in her hand, and I am about ten months old."

We would expect this person to have adopted a style of life in which family ties played a strong part. Such was, in fact, the case. She had assumed the role of mother towards a crippled brother with whom she shared a house. She had received an offer of marriage, which she had hesitated to accept because it involved her in a mental conflict over her obligation to support her brother.

A third example is that of a man who recalled his first day at school. "My mother took me there," he said, "and when she left me I felt that she didn't want me and was just trying to get rid of me." This man's general attitude to life could be summed up in the words: "I feel unwanted." In his social and working life he acted on the assumption that others rejected him. Feeling "odd man out," he created numerous difficulties for himself in his relations with other people.

Consider the following: "Charging the other kids in the orphanage a marble each to watch me act in little plays I'd written." What kind of person would we expect to report this as his or her earliest memory? Obviously, someone to whom an audience and acting were important, perhaps someone who would make the stage a career. According to the press, this is, in fact, the earliest memory of actress Shirley Ann Field.

A man recalled memories of happenings mostly in the chemical laboratory at his secondary school. "Some hydrogen gas caught fire," he said. "I broke some glass apparatus; a fellow student was burned with nitric acid; another chap tasted some chemical material which he thought afterwards might have been phosphorus. What a state he got himself into from the fear of this!" These memories suggest that his interest in chemistry and chemical experiments had played a prominent part in his life. It does not, in fact, surprise us to learn that he was an industrial chemist.

An elderly woman recalled a memory from her seventh birthday when her grandmother gave her a flower and insects from it got on her pinafore, causing her to run back to her granny for help to get rid of them.

Why should this particular memory be recalled from among the thousands of experiences which the lady had had in the last sixty or so years? Because it crystallised, as it were, her attitude towards life in general.

This was confirmed by the lady herself, who admitted: "I have always been a mother to others and have been there to solve their troubles." She recalled the memory because it crystallised the fact that she had been cast in the role of a motherly figure to whom others had appealed for help. Her grandmother's behaviour had perhaps been for her a kind of pattern on which she had modelled her own behaviour.

Another woman recalled that as a child of five she wanted to wear a piece of jewellery belonging to her older sister. She got into a tantrum when her sister insisted on wearing the jewellery and her father threatened to give her a good hiding for being naughty.

It would not be surprising to find that jealousy of her sister had played a prominent part in this woman's emotional life. Such, in fact, turned out to be the case. "You are right," she said, "when you say that strong emotions are tied up with my relationship with my sister. I was very jealous of her boy friends."

Yet another woman recorded three childhood memories as follows:

1. "I am about a year old. I am in a baby's high chair, being fed from a spoon. A nannie wearing a cloak with red on it is bending over me. I feel frightened because I wonder whether she is a nurse or whether it is blood on her cloak."
2. "I am about four and am being dragged by the arm into a room to see my grandmother in her coffin. I am screaming in terror and struggling to escape."
3. "I am about six. A nurse is protesting at my presence in the bedroom where my father is lying ill after an operation. I become terrified and ask to leave."

These memories have a common theme. It is that the young child is frightened by something she doesn't understand. In the first one she doesn't understand whether it is a red cloak or blood. In the second she doesn't understand the mystery of death, and in the third it is the illness and operation which she doesn't understand.

It would not surprise us to find that a person who recalled these memories would be someone who as an adult was still frightened by what she doesn't understand. This is precisely what was found in the present case, because the woman admitted that one of her emotional problems was a fear of the unknown.

"The first thing I remember in life," said Mr. B. C., "was being wrapped in a blanket and carried to an air-raid shelter. I also remember another incident when I was screaming as my drunken father pulled my mother's hair."

These incidents have probably been remembered because they crystallised the sense of insecurity and uncertainty acquired by this man as a result of his childhood experiences, which he described as "so unpleasant."

These feelings were reflected in the casual attitude which he displayed towards work and marriage and indeed towards life in general. "I am twenty-four years of age," he said. "My problem is: what do I want to do in life? I honestly don't know. The weeks drift by uninterestingly. Since leaving school I have had eighteen different jobs, none of which I was interested in. I got married four months ago and am now losing interest in marriage. I don't seem to attach any importance to my marriage; in fact, I don't seem to care whether I am married or not."

All these examples show how a memory survives from childhood because in it is embodied a person's general attitude towards life. But this point of view is applicable not only to memories of actual incidents. It applies equally well to memories of fantasies. That is, if a person recalls from childhood an isolated occasion when he imagined something, what he imagined may be significant for the light it throws upon the kind of person he is.

For example, Mr. S. O. recalled a fantasy dating from the age of seventeen when he was in domestic service to a titled lady. He imagined himself being punished for ignoring her order not to use the front stairs. Why from his past life did he recall this particular fantasy?

The answer is that the memory of the fantasy survived because it crystallised his attitude towards life. We are entitled to assume that an attitude of defiance of authority figured in his make-up at the age of seventeen.

(e) *Disturbance of Memory for Recent Events (Senile Amnesia)*

In discussing infantile amnesia we saw that besides the psychological causes of forgetting, the state of the brain was important. Another period of life in which forgetting is affected by the physiological condition of the body is old age.

As the recording process of memory takes place in the brain, anything that affects the brain must affect the memory. For example, a man was involved in a shooting affray and a bullet grazed his skull, knocking him unconscious. When he recovered he could not even remember the girl who was his fiancée.

There are certain changes in the tissues of the body which are associated with advancing years. They tend to appear progressively when middle life has been passed. Individual persons, however, show wide differences in the date of the appearance and rapidity of evolution of such traits.

One of these traits is a tendency to forget what has just been learned, combined with the absence of impairment of childhood memories. People who are getting on in years may forget events which have occurred a few days, hours or even minutes previously, but they may be able to tell a great deal in detail about the distant past and their childhood.

For example, a man of sixty said: "I find it difficult to remember what I have read, or the details of a transaction, even immediately afterwards, and this leads to errors of all kinds. Yet I can repeat correctly hymns and poems learned in childhood."

This phenomenon may also be observed in connection with many organic brain disturbances, such as senile dementia, brain lesions and tumours, and chronic alcoholic poisoning. It is called the Korsakoff syndrome.

Very often the memory gaps are filled in by "memories" invented either spontaneously or when the patients are asked about their past. In the content of these confabulations Korsakoff found a strong preference for deaths and funerals, although often the content concerned everyday routine.

A pronounced disturbance of memory for recent events will mean that the patients become completely disoriented. This leads them to give some year in the last century as the date, to consider themselves young even if they are well advanced in years, or to mistake the identity of persons around them.

(f) *Déjà Vu*

An unusual and fascinating type of remembering—or forgetting —is the experience known as false recognition or *déjà vu* ("already seen"). It is, says Freud, "that strange feeling we

perceive in certain moments and situations when it seems as if
we had already had exactly the same experience, or had previously
found ourselves in the same situation. Yet we are never successful
in our efforts to recall clearly those former experiences and
situations." (18)

For example, a young man said: "At my work I'll be doing a
certain job and suddenly I feel I have done this particular job in
exactly the same way and in exactly the same conditions some time
long before, when actually I haven't."

"Occasionally," said another young man, "when at a dance or
at work or in other situations I feel that the whole thing has
happened to me before and sometimes I can vaguely sense what is
going to happen. This lasts for only a few minutes at a time."

"During the last six months," added a third person, "I have
been in several situations which I think I have been in before
although I know I haven't. For example, I notice a book open at
a certain page. I feel that I expected to see it open at that place.
I expect my boss to ask me a certain question. This he does and for
the next few minutes everything happens as though I had gone
through the same experience before. This has happened several
times."

Yet another person described an experience of *déjà vu* as follows:
"Last year a friend of mine spent his holidays abroad and paid a
visit to a city he had never read about or heard very much of. As
soon as he arrived there he appeared to be quite conversant with
his surroundings. He found his way to his hotel without being
directed by anyone, without looking at street names. As he put it,
'I just kept on walking until I saw an hotel which I "recognised"
as the one where I was to stay.' When he went to his room, this
again was quite familiar to him; he knew where everything was
placed in it and it seemed to him as if he'd been there all his life.
I suggested that he had read about it or spent some time in his
past in very similar surroundings. He had tried to find an explanation along these lines, but could think of nothing in his experience
to warrant any such solution."

Déjà vu is described by Dickens in one of his novels where he
writes: "Sometimes we get the feeling as if what we say and do has
already been said and done a long time ago, and as if we had seen
the same faces, objects and conditions in primeval times, as if we

could expect what will now be said, and as if we would suddenly remember this." The quality of familiarity and inability to recall the previous experience thus characterise *déjà vu*.

What is the explanation of this feeling that we have already experienced something before, although we know that this is impossible?

It is sometimes thought that the experience confirms the theory of reincarnation. That is to say, what is now experienced is familiar because it has actually been experienced before—in a previous incarnation. Psychology is unable to accept this explanation, which Freud describes as "naïvely mystical and unpsychological."

Those who have read Shaw Desmond's *Reincarnation for Everyman* will recall that a number of cases, including the author's own, are used in it to defend the reincarnation hypothesis.

For example, Shaw Desmond describes in the following words the clear-cut memories that he claims to have of a former life in Rome as a gladiator in the reign of the Emperor Nero:

> "I remembered the men I had fought. I recalled something of their technique. And, above all, I remembered the great Nero himself—he who for me . . . is more real than almost anyone I have known in this life.
>
> "As a child, I heard again the swish of the sling of the Balearic slingers of death and the whine of the stone. Again and again I would practise childishly with my wooden sword as I had once wielded the sword in the arena."

The same author remembers being killed in the arena by his adversary:

> "The man, Clistris, who did me to death that day, I met as a boy in Ireland in my native town, and instantly knew him for what he was . . ." (19)

If it rejects the above explanation, what alternatives has psychology to offer? There are several. One psychological explanation is simply that we have already been to the place we now recognise but have forgotten doing so.

For example, a woman said: "I spent a few days at the French Channel coast resort of Wimereux, near Boulogne, where I got the most intense feeling that I had been there before, although I couldn't remember having done so. I wasn't able to convince myself that I had been there until one day after returning from my holiday I came across by accident a very old hotel bill, which showed that I had spent a week there thirty years ago."

Another explanation is that the present experience reminds you of some incident or situation which resembles it but which you have now forgotten. The present experience reawakens the memory of the previous experience buried in your unconscious mind. You thus feel as though you were recognising something instead of experiencing it for the first time. The past experience has been largely forgotten, but the resemblance leads to the feeling that "it has happened before."

For example, a man and his wife were motoring through New England when they came to a village which he recognised as having seen before, although he knew and his wife agreed that he had never been there. The explanation was that when he was a child his family had had a maid who came from a farm near the village and who had talked incessantly to the boy about her home but he had forgotten it.

"The process of forgetting," says Professor Edward Stevens Robinson of Yale University, "sometimes leads us to recognise that which we have never before experienced. This is probably because we have experienced something like the happening in question, but have so nearly forgotten it that we are unable to tell the difference between the partially remembered happening and that which is falsely recognised."

A third explanation is that what you now believe you have seen or done before is actually something which you have seen or done before in your imagination and which you have stored in your unconscious mind. The original fantasy of seeing or doing it has been repressed, so that you have remained unaware of it. The only evidence of its existence is the feeling of familiarity that now strikes you. This is created by the fact that you are now doing something which you have already imagined yourself doing.

For example, a soldier said: "When I put on a black dress uniform and looked at myself in the mirror, I had a funny feeling as if I had done it before, yet I knew I hadn't." The explanation was that about nine months previously he had imagined how smart he would look in such a uniform.

Freud accepts this explanation. He considers the *déjà vu* phenomenon to be based on the memory of an unconscious fantasy. The feeling of familiarity can be referred to fantasies of which we are unconsciously reminded in an actual situation.

For example, a woman told him that as a child of twelve she had visited the house of some friends in the country. There she was struck by the feeling that she had seen everything before, although she knew that this was the first visit she had paid to it. The explanation was that a few months before her visit she had had to leave home and stay with relatives on account of the illness of her only brother. Unconsciously she had hoped that when she returned home she would find that her brother had died and that she would be restored to the centre of the family stage. However, her brother did not die and the thought remained repressed. A few months later, when she visited the home of her friends, she found that their brother, too, was ill. This similarity between their home and her own revived the memory of her unconscious fantasy and created the sense of familiarity which she experienced.

"I believe," writes Freud, "that it is wrong to designate the feeling of having experienced something before as an illusion. On the contrary, in such moments, something is really touched that we have already experienced, only we cannot consciously recall the latter because it never was conscious. In the latter, the feeling of *déjà vu* corresponds to the memory of an unconscious fantasy." (20)

When a long-past dream is stirred by some new occurrence, it, too, may cause this false recognition. For example, a man said: "I get a feeling when I am in a strange place or faced with an unusual situation, that I have been there before, or coped with the situation before, when in reality I know I haven't! Would you infer that I have probably dreamed of this strange place or unusual situation at a previous date?"

The *déjà vu* experience occurs not only in waking life but it can also occur in dreams. This is illustrated by the following report of a woman who said: "In my dreams I tend to get into situations which I feel I have been in before."

The following dream throws light on the origin of the *déjà vu* experience. A young man said: "I dreamed of a large house with a garden and a drive. I remembered it so vividly that I am sure I could recognise the place if I ever saw it." If this young man were to forget this dream but later on to see a house which resembled the dream-house, he might well experience the feeling of familiarity characteristic of *déjà vu*.

CHAPTER 3

HOW TO REMEMBER

HAVING established what the causes of forgetting are, we should now be in a position to suggest how they can be removed. Our conclusions on this point should yield us practical hints on making the most effective use of our memory. Incidentally, it should be mentioned, if it has not already been made clear, that what we learn here about both remembering and forgetting is not "armchair" speculation. We are dealing with the scientific findings of psychologists based on their laboratory experiments.

First of all, let us recapitulate what we learned in Chapter 2. We discovered that the causes of forgetting are:

1. Getting a weak impression by not attending to an experience properly.
2. Letting the impression fall into disuse by failure to repeat it.
3. Interference from other impressions.
4. Repression of unpleasant memories.

This analysis shows us what we need to do to avoid or stop such causes. This is, in fact, all that the practical problem of memory amounts to. In order to reduce or remove the causes of forgetting and so be able to remember better, we have to:

1. Get a strong impression by paying careful attention.
2. Repeat under conditions in which repetition is effective.
3. Avoid or reduce interference as much as possible.
4. Lift the repression or avoid it forming.

It will be the purpose of the present chapter to try to show how each of these aims may be accomplished.

1. IMPRESSION

The first cause of a poor memory is getting a weak impression of the thing we wish to remember. Getting a strong impression of it means attending to it properly or concentrating on it.

We must obtain a deep impression on the mind of what we wish to remember. The attention must be concentrated on one thing only at a time to the exclusion of everything else.

At any given time various impressions converge upon the mind. A selection among them is effected by attention, which is the directing of mental activity towards a mental or physical object or situation. Attending to something consists in putting oneself into such a relation with it as to gain the fullest possible experience from it.

In every such mental process a certain amount of concentration is necessary. Concentration is, in fact, sustained attention. Hence we must understand certain facts about this process if we are to improve our power of concentration.

Attention is constantly shifting. Even when one is concentrating, attention shifts rapidly from one aspect to another of the matter to which we are attending. Some people claim to be able to carry on two or more activities at the same time. What really happens is that their attention changes continuously and rapidly from one to the other.

We cannot continue indefinitely to attend to one thing if no new focus of interest is introduced. If forced beyond this point, natural sleep or an hypnotic state ensues. This is, in fact, the principle which the hypnotist uses in putting his subject "under the influence."

We cannot concentrate on one object for any considerable length of time without an effort of will. When we listen to a monotonous speaker, our attention wanders to other matters and has to be recalled. A single object or situation cannot hold attention for very long unless it has many details, such as a painting. Thus a thought cannot usually be retained for a long time before other thoughts interrupt. This lack of constancy is found especially in children. In adults there are great individual differences with respect to it. These also depend on the kind of object observed and the individual interest in it.

The problem of attention and concentration is really the problem of habit. We must develop the habit of paying attention to what concerns us. With practice we can learn to disregard many things which at first strongly attract our attention. If we lived within the sound of Niagara Falls, we should probably learn in time to ignore it. We can also learn to pay attention to some things which might otherwise be neglected, e.g. the ticking of a clock in a room full of the buzz of conversation.

Attention may be voluntary or involuntary. Voluntary attention is the result of forming the habit of attending. It is directed towards an object or idea by one's own decision backed by an effort of will. Involuntary attention, on the other hand, is brought about by the intensity of the impression or by the interest which it arouses.

Voluntary attention is fixed by an effort of will on some object which does not in itself interest us. The interest lies in some indirect object, as, for example, when one studies a dull subject in order to pass an examination.

If you want to concentrate on something, you must feel that it matters to you. You must be interested in it. It must evoke your enthusiasm. The deeper and more permanent the interest the more sustained the attention.

Without the interest that brings involuntary attention, an effort of will is necessary. This is bound to mean some degree of tension. If, however, the tension is too strong, it will distract us from what we are trying to concentrate on. We must strike a balance between relaxation and tension.

The distribution of attention is inversely proportional to its intensity. That is to say, if we concentrate intently on one object, other objects are observed to a lesser degree. Concentration can be disturbed by distracting impressions, especially those of emotional value, the strength of which increases the distraction. For example, a teacher said: "I have begun work for an Arts degree but find great difficulty in concentrating because of my self-consciousness which is always before me."

It will thus be seen that the problem of concentration lies in (a) forming the habit of bringing the mind back every time it wanders; (b) acquiring a deep and permanent interest in the matter to which we are seeking to attend; (c) relaxing our tension until we are slightly braced up but not too much; and (d) settling any emotional problems which distract our attention from what we are doing.

In other words, concentration depends upon four things:

Habit, Interest, Relaxation and Emotion. These points may be remembered by summarising them in the word HIRE.

Before passing on to consider each of them in greater detail, we are now in a position to say something about the value of attention. This will be seen when we realise that attention is the first step in all the higher mental processes. Its selective nature enables us to construct an orderly world out of the mass of sense impressions. The shifting of attention greatly facilitates one's adjustment to the environment. As soon as one aspect of the environment is fully comprehended, one's attention almost invariably shifts to another.

The improvement of concentration is a benefit sometimes claimed to result from the use of a particular brand of advertised product. The psychologist, however, must struggle on with such techniques of improving concentration as he has found of value.

(a) *Habit*

The inability to concentrate is often a sign that a person is the victim of over-indulgence in fantasy, which, when conscious, takes the form of day-dreaming. The law of attention is that we can attend to only one thing at once. While we are attending to our fantasies, we cannot concentrate upon anything else.

Many persons complain of "lack of concentration" or "bad memory." It may at first sight appear that they are right, but in reality they are complaining about their day-dreams. These so engross their attention as not to permit concentration. To concentrate under these circumstances requires an effort of will to check unconscious fantasy that runs counter to what we are trying to study.

Another factor plays a role in this condition. Our day-dreams are, as a rule, emotionally charged. On the other hand, study material with its relatively low emotional charge is often unable to attract a great amount of our attention. The student, therefore, prefers to indulge in day-dreams. Because he does not attend to what he seeks to learn, he does not remember it, and, therefore, he believes that he has a poor memory.

For example, a student said: "I am above average in my studies, but my problem is that I lack concentration when reading. My mind wanders away on to thoughts of sex."

This man's mind is distracted from what he wishes to attend to by fantasies arising from the pressure of his natural instincts. Whilst he is attending to his fantasies or day-dreams, he cannot concentrate upon the subject he is reading, and unless a person concentrates he cannot expect to remember.

On the other hand, it would be a mistake to think that concentration is the full answer to the problem of memory. That something more besides is necessary is illustrated by the following report. A man said: "I find it difficult to remember things that have been said to me, although I concentrate on what I am being told at the time." Nevertheless, it cannot be denied that concentration is essential to memory, even if other conditions must be met as well.

Concentration is a habit and habits are perfected by practice. William James said: "There is no such thing as voluntary, sustained attention for more than a few seconds at a time. What is called sustained, voluntary attention, is a repetition of successive efforts which bring back the topic to the mind."

We must persevere in trying to concentrate until we succeed. Habit is as strong a force for good as for ill. We should try to build up habits that are conducive to concentration. For instance, it helps to sit down to work at a definite time and in a definite place.

If your mind tends to wander to other things, bring it back gently each time to what you are doing. Other thoughts tend to intrude because this is the normal way in which the mind works, one thought succeeding another. The technique of concentrating "goes against the grain" and may, therefore, require some practice before it succeeds. Persistent practice of this kind will eventually enable you to develop the habit of concentration.

When you find it hard to concentrate, the thoughts that crowd into your mind are not unimportant. If they push out what you are trying to study, they must be more important than the latter. In fact, they may contain a key to your most important problems. They may be your mind's way of advising you to "put first things first."

For example, a young teacher complained: "I find it very hard to concentrate and apply myself properly to my studies." Invited to give details of the thoughts that passed through his mind while studying, he replied: "There is always some girl in my mind. I picture myself making advances to her. I think of myself in some heroic position with a girl admiring me."

These thoughts show that the young man's real problem is not his difficulty in concentrating but his sexual frustration. The tendency to rely upon fantasy for compensation will diminish as his life situation brings him greater satisfaction in the world of reality. Always begin by dealing with your most important problem, and then you will find that concentration is no trouble at all.

(b) *Interest*

A man said: "When I listen to a person talking to me about something uninteresting, my mind wanders. I want to improve my concentration. Can you tell me how?"

This report illustrates that concentration depends upon interest in what we are doing. This man's mind wanders from what is being said because, as he himself admits, he finds it uninteresting.

The law of interest is of paramount importance in concentrating. Interest means to be in the midst of a situation. Unless interest is present, unless one throws oneself heart and soul into a thing, concentration becomes extremely difficult or even impossible without a deliberate effort of will. And while the individual is attending to willing himself to concentrate, he cannot attend to what he is trying to concentrate on.

Interest is the pleasure derived from the harmonious co-existence of a present impression and one which has been perceived previously. This psychological process also arouses a sense of familiarity, and attention is then directed towards the impression, selecting it from a number of other objects.

We must develop and build an interest in whatever we would mentally retain. Things in which we are deeply interested will be remembered without conscious effort. As a private secretary put it: "I do not forget anything that is vital to me."

For example, a boy who is interested in planes or trains easily recognises the different types he "spots," because his interest has led him to study them. On the other hand, to the person who has no special interest in them one plane or locomotive is apt to look very much like another.

Another example which illustrates the dependence of memory upon interest is the following. A man said: "For certain things my memory is very good. Usually they are memories tied up with my interests. Some people are quite surprised on occasions when I can recall instances where they have either said or done something which they had forgotten. I can remember a colleague's surprise as she was going through a list of some musical shows and operatic works she had seen—but she had forgotten a rarer work which she definitely had seen—Bizet's 'Pearl Fishers.' It had been a few years since she had mentioned seeing this work but her interest in opera was not so keen as mine. It was therefore much to her surprise when I remembered something that was really part of her own memory."

If we have to attend to something in spite of its being un-interesting, we can improve our concentration by strengthening our interest. This can be done in the following way. The practical remedy for the difficulty is to repeat to ourselves: "This interests me and I'll remember it," or "This work is interesting me more and more," or "This subject is useful to me and I like it more each day."

In other words, to stimulate interest where it is flagging, or to cultivate it where it is lacking altogether, make use of the simple method of autosuggestion. The value of this advice may be judged from the following reports made by persons who applied it and found it beneficial.

"This method has helped a lot to overcome my inability to concentrate," said a student. "Now when I read I take in about twice as much as I did previously."

Another person who complained of lack of concentration reported: "My power of concentration has greatly improved. When I was reading, my mind would just wander away, but now I can concentrate on a subject because it interests me."

Concentration and memory, however, do not depend entirely upon interest. Interest by itself will not ensure a person being able to concentrate and remember. This may be noted from the following reports.

"I find great difficulty in remembering things I have read," said a housewife, *even though I take a great interest in them*."

"I don't seem as though I can concentrate," said a salesman, "no matter how hard I try. It's not because I am not interested. I am indeed full of enthusiasm about the work."

This illustrates an important point about interest. One must really be interested in a thing *for its own sake* in order to be able to concentrate on it. This man was not really interested in his work for its own sake. His real difficulty was not lack of concentration but self-consciousness. He was interested in his work because he thought that it promised him a means of convincing himself that he had overcome his self-consciousness.

Here are three further examples that illustrate this important point.

A woman said: "I am tone-deaf. Apparently this slight physical defect has been with me all my life. It seems to me that owing to it I have never really listened properly to anything or anybody, and if I read my powers of concentration are not at all good. Do you think I could make myself listen to talks on the radio if I really concentrated?"

What she appears to be saying to herself is: "If I listened to talks on the radio, it would prove that I was able to concentrate." However, this is not the best motive for listening to radio talks. The proper motive for doing this is that you are interested in the subject of the talk.

A man said: "I am studious-minded and have spent a lot on postal tuition, but whenever I try to study I fail to concentrate and fall asleep."

This man may be trying to study because he thinks that success in that line would give him a good opinion of himself or give other people a good opinion of him. Such a motive, however, is not a satisfactory substitute for a genuine interest in the subject-matter of the lessons. This interest may be absent in his case and, if so, it would explain why he is unable to concentrate and tends to escape into sleep.

There are two ways of solving this problem. One is that he should give up his studies and find some other way of spending his time. The other is to cultivate a genuine interest in the actual subject-matter of the lessons. This can be attempted on the lines shown above.

Here is another example of a man who was doing the right thing for the wrong reasons. He said: "I want to study for my G.C.E.

in five subjects, but find great difficulty in settling down and concentrating properly. I have been studying on and off for about five years, but have made little progress. I think that, because I did not get my School Certificate at school, I have had a secret inferiority complex. If I had some qualification, it would be a spur to further ambition."

His real problem is that he feels inferior. He no doubt believes that if he were to obtain his G.C.E., it would give him a better opinion of himself. It would enable him to feel the equal of or even superior to some other people who do not possess the G.C.E.

The snag is that this motive will not in itself sustain his studies of five subjects. He can do this only if he is interested in the subjects for their own sake. If you are going to study, say, English Literature or Mathematics or French, you must have a keen interest in these branches of knowledge themselves. This may be what he lacks and, if so, it explains his difficulty in getting down to his studies.

In other words, you should study algebra, or Latin or history, or whatever it is, because you think that they are worth studying— not because of what you think the possession of a G.C.E. can do for you.

If he can discover within himself a genuine interest in his subjects as subjects, this man should be able to obtain his G.C.E. On the other hand, if he is not interested in the subjects for their own sake, he would be wise to get into some other occupation where he can make progress without possessing a G.C.E.

(c) *Relaxation*

What is the relation between concentration and relaxation? Is concentration assisted by relaxing or by tensing? This seems to be a matter of debate.

One opinion favours the view that concentration occurs most naturally when body and mind are relaxed. According to this view, the ideal means of concentrating would be to sit down in a relaxed posture. That is to say, the person who is concentrating is not all keyed up and tense, but relaxed and confident.

For example, a bank clerk said: "I make mistakes because I am trying too hard to concentrate. I find it very difficult to concentrate at all, as I am unable to relax. I think it would be a great help if I were."

Relaxation should not, of course, be confused with fatigue. Little is gained by attempting to concentrate when one is tired. "My main trouble is overwork," said a forty-year-old widow. "When I do sit down to study I am too tired to concentrate."

On the other hand, there are those who favour the view that concentration means tension, not relaxation. Jacobsen, author of *Progressive Relaxation*, states that mental activity in general diminishes as muscular relaxation progresses. "With progressive muscular relaxation," he writes, "attention, thought-processes, and emotion gradually diminish." He concludes that "the experience of muscular tenseness" is a necessary requirement of attention. (21)

Muensterberg, too, believed that concentration demands muscular tension. He formulated what is known as the action theory, which maintains that the strength of our attention, or perhaps better, its vividness, when, e.g., looking at an object, depends on the openness of the paths in the nervous system leading to the muscles. When these paths are not wholly clear, the object we are perceiving or the words we are listening to will not register fully in consciousness. To attend will, therefore, require a certain muscular tension or preparedness.

Robert H. Thouless advocates "a position in which the muscles are braced up" as favourable to concentration. Yet he admits that "keeping the muscles tense is not the same thing as mental concentration and is not even essential to it, and it has the objection that it is fatiguing in itself."

This controversy on the merits of relaxation *v*. tension for concentration has now been settled by Courts.

In Courts's experiment sixty college students learned nonsense syllables while exerting muscular effort by squeezing a dynamometer. A nonsense syllable consists of a vowel between two consonants, e.g. zek. A dynamometer is an instrument designed to measure strength of grip. Each subject squeezed the dynamometer as hard as he could in order to measure the strength of his maximum grip. Then he learned lists of syllables both without squeezing the dynamometer and also while squeezing it at different strengths up to his maximum grip. When the subjects were tested on how much they had learned, it was shown that the number of syllables which they recalled increased up to the point where they were exerting a quarter of their maximum grip. Beyond that point the number of syllables recalled began to fall off, until by the time they were exerting three-quarters of their maximum grip they actually recalled less than they did without the dynamometer at all.

The conclusion to be drawn from this experiment is that *a slight amount of tension improves learning, but a larger amount diminishes it*. (22)

(d) *Worry or Emotional Conflict*

A young man said: "I find difficulty in concentrating. Whenever I am reading or attending lectures, my mind wanders. I am beginning to worry about it, because, unless I put all my mind into my work, there are scant chances of passing examinations."

"The normal person concentrates on what seems to him important," says Dr. Sigmund Freud, "in the way of an impression or a piece of work in order that it shall not be interfered with by the intrusion of any other mental processes or activities." (23)

When it is interfered with, as in the above case, this is often a sign that a person is the victim of emotional conflict. This more than anything else interferes with the process of sustained attention.

The *law of attention*, which we noted earlier, is that *one cannot attend to two things at once*, or that *two or more things cannot be done with equal intensity*. A man reading his programme as he watches a play seems to be able to attend to both at the same time. The truth of the matter, however, is that his attention alternates rapidly between the two.

The inability to attend may be due to worry about one's other problems. While you are attending to your problems or worries, you cannot concentrate upon anything else. For example, of a group of college students who were referred for psychiatric aid on account of reading disabilities, half were found to have emotional difficulties. The most common included feelings of inferiority and insecurity, immature personalities, depression and poor social adaptation. (24)

This means that lack of concentration may not be the main problem. It may merely point to the existence of some other problem that requires to be solved. When this has been done, there should be no further difficulty in concentrating, for the attention will then no longer be divided between the worrying problem and the effort to concentrate.

The truth of this statement is borne out time and again by persons who at first complain of being unable to concentrate and afterwards admit that they don't like their jobs or that some other difficulty needs to be put right.

For example, a student who at first submitted lack of concentration as his problem, was afterwards found to be a partner to a broken marriage. When he had solved his marital difficulties, his inability to concentrate disappeared without requiring to be treated as a separate problem.

A man complained: "I am hampered by a poor power of concentration. I cannot keep my mind from wandering." Later he made the following disclosure: "Actually it was a case of worrying. When you state that my lack of concentration is due to emotional conflict, you are perfectly correct. I am living with a woman for whom I have not the slightest affection. We have a boy of two to whom I am devoted. My lawful wife, whom I deserted, is prepared to take me back. I want to return to her but cannot leave my baby, whom the mother will not give to me."

Another man also complained of difficulty in concentrating. His real problem, which he did not reveal until fifteen months later, was that he was a homosexual. "I was a fool," he admitted, "to think that any problem was too private to disclose, or too anti-social for you to attend to, and so I kept quiet about the one serious problem I had and still have."

The principle that the student should follow for improving his concentration is to seek out and remove the real difficulty responsible for it, and not to expect to be able to concentrate until he has done so. You should face up to your emotional problems, and do what you can to solve them if they can be solved, or accept them and learn to live with them if they cannot be solved.

The fourth rule for improving one's powers of concentration is, therefore, to attend either to the matter in hand, or, if that is not possible, to one's worries with a view to eliminating them, but do not expect to be able to attend to both at once.

Summary of Advice on How to Concentrate

Let us now summarise what we have learned about the causes of poor concentration and how to eliminate them. We have learned that lack of concentration is caused by the habit of day-dreaming, lack of interest in the subject, too little or too much muscular tension, and worry or emotional conflict, which distracts attention from what we are doing.

This means that we must acquire the habit of concentration by bringing our mind back every time it wanders to other things. We must strengthen our interest in the subject by repeating to ourselves, "This work is interesting me more and more." A slight degree of muscular tension is needed, but not too much. The ideal means of concentrating is to sit down in a lightly braced posture. Finally, we should try to deal with any emotional problems that we have. A quiet mind is the best guarantee of concentration.

In overcoming inattention we learn to concentrate. We thus deal with the first cause of a poor memory, i.e. the original experience not making a strong enough impression on us. Better concentration means a stronger impression, and the more vivid the impression the easier it is recalled.

Before passing on to consider the second cause of a poor memory and what can be done to eradicate it, we must note that the attention we are asked to give should be active and not passive, i.e., we should make a definite resolve to remember what we are paying attention to.

Attending without actively resolving to remember is of little use. For example, a man said: "I remembered a person quite well—his voice, the circumstances of our meeting, etc., but not his name, for I did not make any serious attempt to commit his name to memory at the time."

A psychologist was able to memorise a list of nonsense syllables after repeating them only nine times, when he made up his mind to learn them. When he did not make up his mind to learn them but merely repeated them parrot fashion (passive attention), he required eighty-nine repetitions to memorise a similar list.

(25)

Another man recalled the following memory, which at the time of its occurrence had been accompanied by the intention to remember it:

"One winter, when I was about eight, I was sledging in the late evening down a slope outside our house. The pleasure was such that I wished it would never end. The only flaw in my happiness was the certain knowledge that one of my parents would shortly come to the gate and call me in. As I careered downhill for the umpteenth time, I became aware that I had a spectator. My father was standing at the gate. He smiled but did not call me. I went downhill twice more and then made for the gate, my sledge bumping up the steps after me. As we went in together I thought: 'I will always remember this evening,' and I always have."

A woman said: "I cannot remember book titles very well unless I make a special effort. If I read a book which I am not likely to pick up again, I have no sooner put it down than the title has gone from me. It is the same with films."

This experience, too, illustrates the part played in remembering by the resolve to remember. She did not remember the title of a book or film because, not being interested in reading or seeing it again, she did not make a conscious resolve to remember it.

Therefore, don't be content merely to attend to what you are doing, but study it with the conscious intention to remember it. Make up your mind that you will remember it. Memory is assisted by the intention to remember. What you will to remember you actually do remember.

2. REPETITION

In an experimental proof of the effectiveness of repetition a number of radio scripts were prepared in two versions. In one version the material was presented straightforwardly without repetition. In the other the main points were repeated several times. Both versions were read to each group of the audience taking part in the experiment. After each script had been read the members of the audience answered questions on its factual content and were also asked to say how well they had understood the passage.

When the main points of a script were repeated the material was both understood and remembered better than when there was no repetition. "Repetition facilitates comprehension and aids memory," conclude the authors of the experiment. (26)

We have noted that attention is most effective when accompanied by the resolve to remember. There are also certain conditions under which repetition is most effective. Merely repeating what we wish to remember does not in itself ensure that we remember it, although, of course, we cannot be expected to remember it unless we do repeat it.

Psychologists have discovered a number of conditions under which repeating what we wish to remember helps us to remember it. Some of these conditions, which we will examine in the present section, are as follows:

(a) You remember better if you understand what you repeat.
(Comprehension)
(b) You remember better if you study a little but often.
(Spaced learning)
(c) You remember better if you recite to yourself.
(Recitation)
(d) You remember better if you repeat for longer than you need to learn. (Overlearning)
(e) You remember better if you repeat wholes rather than parts.
(Whole learning)
(f) You remember better if you tell yourself that you can.
(Autosuggestion)
(g) You remember better under conditions like those under which you learned. (Reintegration)
(h) You remember uncompleted tasks better than completed ones. (Zeigarnik effect)
This holds true unless you are afraid of failure or concerned about success, when you may remember a completed task better than an uncompleted one.
(i) You remember better something that contrasts with its background. (von Restorff effect)

Let us describe and illustrate each of these conditions in turn.

(a) *The Law of Comprehension* (*Memory and Meaning*)

What is the law of comprehension? It is: to remember—

understand. The law states a fact of common experience. This is that the better we understand what we learn, the better we remember it. Meaningful material is better retained or more readily relearned than nonsense or rote material. The more meaning any material has the more easily it is memorised and the less rapidly it is forgotten. For example, Ebbinghaus showed that, after they had been learned, relatively fewer repetitions were required to relearn eighty-syllable stanzas of "Don Juan" than to relearn a twelve-syllable nonsense list. (27) A conscious intention must be made to memorise relatively meaningless material. This is just as well; otherwise our minds would be cluttered with useless information.

You can make practical use of this law if you clearly comprehend what you want to remember; if the meaning is not clear it is difficult to remember it. The very effort to find a meaning will stimulate attention and fix the material more firmly in the memory. "The more you know about a thing," writes Dr. Henry Knight Miller in *Practical Psychology*, "the easier it is to remember. *Always try to understand*." (28)

Try to gain insight into the general principles that govern the skill or knowledge you wish to acquire. Keep your mind open for new meanings. If you fail to see them, however, put the problem on one side. You cannot force a solution and prolonged "trial and error" is wasteful. Return to the problem later on when insight may come with little effort.

Thorndike formulated the above principle in another way as the law of belongingness, which states that items integrated into a pattern are better remembered than those which merely occur in close proximity. Christian names and surnames, for example, appear to "go together" and may be better learned than a series of pairs of Christian names. Subjects and predicates go together. The law of belongingness also refers to seeing the relations between the part and the whole.

The value of comprehension is underlined by the following experiment. Two classes of pupils were asked to learn these numbers:

581215192226

293336404347

The first class was told that both numbers were built up on the same principle and that they could remember the numbers by discovering the principle. The principle is that of adding 3 and then 4, i.e., 5 plus 3 = 8, 8 plus 4 = 12, etc.

Then the second class was told to learn the numbers by grouping them in threes and they were written on the blackboard in the following fashion:

$$581 \quad 215 \quad 192 \quad 226$$
$$293 \quad 336 \quad 404 \quad 347$$

Twenty-three per cent of Class I, who had memorised by understanding, were able to remember both numbers correctly three weeks later, while not one of the second class was able to do so.

This clearly shows that we remember best what has meaning for us, or, at least, we may remember it better than what has little or no meaning for us. (29)

(b) *Spaced Learning* ("*Little and Often*")

Which is the better method of studying a correspondence course —thirty minutes every day or two hours every three or four days?

The better method is to spend thirty minutes every day. A short period of study each day is better than a longer period every now and then.

Ebbinghaus found that material which he learned by practice spaced over several days was better remembered than material learned by practice massed on one day. (30)

Mr. S. L. said: "I study only at week-ends because during the week I am too busy." It must be admitted that this is not an ideal method of study. After a week he has probably forgotten most of what was studied the previous week-end.

Instead of spending an hour or two once a week he would do better to spread the same time over seven days. This helps to keep the material fresh in mind and to get the best out of one's studies. This man did, in fact, adopt the suggestion. Up to that point his average mark per lesson for his written work had been 77 per cent. After his attention had been drawn to the value of spaced learning, his average mark per lesson rose to 92 per cent.

"As in music, which I am also studying," he added, "daily practice should be the rule, and from now on I intend to make time for it."

In a psychological experiment, substituting letters for numbers was memorised nearly twice as well in six twenty-minute periods as in one period of two hours. 135 letters were substituted for numbers in the two-hour practice period as compared with 195 letters in three forty-minute periods, 255 letters in six twenty-minute periods, and 265 letters in twelve ten-minute periods. In other words, when the same amount of time was broken up or spaced into six practice periods, the results were almost twice as good as when it was spent in one period. (31)

Another experiment compared three methods of spacing twenty-four repetitions of lists of nonsense syllables. When the learners were tested, six repetitions a day for four days yielded a higher score than eight repetitions a day for three days. A still higher score was achieved, however, from two repetitions a day for twelve days. That is to say, the longer the period over which the repetitions were spaced, the greater the amount that was remembered. (32)

"Similar work has also been done with sensible material—prose or poetry—to be learned," writes Dr. Francis Aveling; "and the same general advantage of 'spaced out' over continuous learning has been established here."

In acquiring a skill, too, daily practice is superior to longer but less frequent practice. This is illustrated by an experiment in which drawing a star while looking in a mirror was mastered better in short daily periods than in longer periods on alternate days. A psychologist compared the progress made by two groups of people. One group practised once at each sitting, which was held every day. The other group practised ten times at each sitting, which was held every other day. At the end of a week the first group had made the same progress as the second group, although the first had practised only seven times as compared with the other group's thirty attempts. (33, 34)

Suppose one is going to have, say, a course of ten driving lessons. Imagine that they are being taken by a person who as yet has no car of his own. Therefore, he will not be getting any practice in the intervals between the lessons. Is it better for him to have one lesson a week for ten weeks or one lesson a day for ten days? In either case he will do the same amount of driving and the cost will be the same. The sole criterion by which to judge between the two methods is the efficiency with which the skill is mastered.

The principle of spaced learning argues in favour of the daily lessons being the more efficient procedure for our learner-driver. In the once-weekly method the skill acquired at each lesson will be largely lost in the intervals between lessons. By contrast, the daily lessons will reinforce that skill before it has time to fall into disuse. Therefore, if practicable, the daily method is to be preferred.

(c) *The Law of Recitation*

The law of recitation states that study material is learned more rapidly when it is recited to oneself or aloud at frequent intervals during memorising.

Instead of continued re-reading of a lesson it is better to recite to yourself what you have learned before you have finished learning it. Interrupt your reading in order to run over what you have learned either by mentally recapitulating the main points or preparing a written summary.

Recitation of the material during learning increases the amount which will be remembered. "If I can read it out aloud," said Miss D. S., "I find it sinks in better."

Why is it better to repeat the material aloud than to rely exclusively on silent reading? There are four reasons: (a) it makes the work more interesting; (b) it makes us pay more attention to it; (c) it enables us to test ourselves; and (d) it utilises the ear, which is as much an aid to learning as the eye.

A well-known laboratory experiment in which students memorised short biographies which they afterwards reproduced has shown that memory is improved when as much as four-fifths of the study time is spent in mentally running over the material without referring to it. Sixty-two per cent of the material was remembered when four-fifths of the learning time was spent in recalling what had been learned in the remaining one-fifth, as against 46 per cent when the whole of the learning period was devoted to reading. (35)

By means of a film strip groups of recruits at a U.S. Army reception centre were taught the phonetic alphabet, e.g., "Able, Baker" for "A, B," etc. Half of the groups recited what they were learning by calling out the phonetic equivalents when they were shown the letters. The other half did no recitation by calling out, but were simply shown the letters with their equivalents. When both groups were tested the former remembered the material better than the latter. (36)

In other experiments on the learning of spelling, arithmetic and French vocabulary the self-recitation method has been proved to be much superior to merely studying and re-studying the material without reciting it. (37, 38)

Reading and re-reading, then, although the commonest, is not the best method of study. It uses only the eye. If you want to remember better, you should use the ear and the muscle sense as well. This can be done by reading aloud or discussing what you read with another person. The muscle sense can be used by making notes on what you read and rewriting the notes, reorganising them in different ways.

A student found lectures interesting, but missed a good deal while taking notes. He therefore decided to prepare a mental outline, writing up the lecture later. This form of recitation enabled him to memorise it.

Another example of the effective use of recitation is as follows. A young law student used to read newspaper reports of trials and then summarise them several times from memory. Each time he would compare his summary with the report, correcting and amending it until he was satisfied he knew it. Eventually he was able to remember the report of a trial after reading it only once. (39)

Dr. Bruno Furst recommends that a similar method be used for learning geography. Draw from memory, he says, a map of a country. Correct your effort after comparing it with an atlas. Again draw the map from memory. Again correct it. When you are satisfied with your map, let a few days pass and then draw another one from memory.

(d) *The Law of Overlearning*

A very good principle to adopt is that of overlearning the material you are studying. Say it over and over again to yourself silently and aloud until you can repeat it several times without making a mistake.

The law of overlearning states that the more thoroughly study material is learned, the longer it is remembered. Material well learned is remembered better than material poorly learned. *Do not repeat what you wish to remember until you barely know it, but until you know it really well.*

A helpful point in remembering a chapter of a book is to go over the outstanding facts in one's mind after closing the book. Think about the subject-matter with a view to reconciling it with what you have learned previously and logically arranging it in your mind for future reference. Adopt the habit of frequently revising the material you have learned. For example, a student reports: "I go over my lessons time and again till I have them off by heart."

The simplest method of remembering names employs this principle of overlearning. Whenever you meet someone, get his or her name correctly. Give your full attention to it when you are introduced. Ask the person to repeat or spell it if you don't catch it the first time. Make a point of repeating the name several times during the course of conversation. For example, don't just say "How do you do?"; say "How do you do, Mrs. Postlethwaite?". Give yourself an incentive to remember their names by taking an interest in people. Associate a particularly difficult name with something else which you can remember. For example, a man whose name was Altkastell invited his friends to think of him as "Oldcastle."

When you think you have memorised a fact, it will repay you to go on repeating it a little longer. You remember a thing better if you continue to study it even after you have thoroughly learned it. Whatever time you spend on learning something, spend half as much time again on overlearning it. Something you learn in ten minutes will be remembered better if you repeat it for another five minutes after you know it.

A group of students repeated lists of nouns until they knew them. Another group repeated them for half as long again. After two weeks the latter group remembered more than four times as much as the former.

The degree of improvement in memory, however, is not uniformly proportional to the number of extra repetitions. A smaller number of extra repetitions is bound to result in an improvement. The further improvement from a large number of repetitions may not justify the time and effort spent on them, unless the material must be remembered perfectly, e.g. when a pianist practises for a concert. (40, 41)

(e) *The Law of Whole Learning*

Generally speaking, material to be learned should be studied as a whole rather than bit by bit.

You will remember something better if you repeat it as a whole over and over again than if you break it up into parts and learn each part separately. The best way to memorise a passage is to keep reciting it in its entirety rather than a few lines at a timel Start with the whole but watch for spots that may call for specia. attention. Select for special practice the parts that are most difficult to learn. If the passage is very long, it should be divided into sections and each section treated as a whole.

For example, learn a poem as a whole rather than one stanza at a time. Read it all through and through until it is mastered rather than divide it into parts and memorise the parts before trying to recite the whole. In the case of poems up to 240 lines in length, the saving of time by the whole method of reading the complete poem through each time may amount to as much as 15 per cent. After the part method of learning a poem verse by verse we must mentally put the whole together at the end; reading the whole poem also adds meaning to the learning.

That is why in learning to play the piano students practise both hands together instead of each hand separately, and why the swimmer practises arm and leg movements together.

Seibert compared two ways of studying French vocabulary: to read through and through the list of words from beginning to end (whole method), or study it a word at a time (part method). When she compared the results of both methods, she found that students who had adopted the former remembered after two days half as much again as students who had studied one word and its French equivalent at a time. (42)

The superiority of the whole method over the part method of learning is further illustrated by the way in which the training of Morse code operators was improved in the United States army during World War II. Originally the code had been taught by the part method, in which the letters of the alphabet and the ten numerals were learned in several groups. The psychologists who were asked to improve the training recommended that the code be learned as a whole. As a result of this and other improvements the rate of failure among soldiers undergoing training was reduced from 15 per cent to 3.4 per cent, and the time required for training radio operators was reduced from between thirty-five and forty-one hours to twenty-seven hours. (43)

My daughter has shown me a religious tract in which the reader is recommended to memorise four scriptural texts as follows: learn the first, then learn the second and revise the first. When you have memorised the first two, learn the third. When you have learned the first three, learn the fourth. It is obvious that this is the part method. The material would probably be learned quicker and remembered better if all four texts were learned together, the reader repeating them all one after the other until they were known.

(f) *The Law of Confidence*

A poor memory can be caused by constantly telling ourselves that our memory is poor.

An attitude of confidence in one's memory tends to make it better than it would otherwise be. Fear, self-consciousness, stage-fright and worry interfere with the process of recalling.

Four patients were told under hypnosis, "You will forget everything about your body when you awaken." Not only were they unable to name parts of their bodies but one patient, for example, found it difficult to name objects and to draw geometrical figures. Another was unable to recognise articles of clothing, and estimated wrongly the length, thickness and parallelism of lines. This study illustrates in a striking way how responsive our memory is to the suggestion that it is poor. If we accept such a suggestion, it will actually tend to make our memory poor. (44)

You can improve your confidence in your memory by means of autosuggestion, repeating to yourself, "Day by day in every way, I remember better and better." Repeat this formula twenty or thirty times when you retire at night, after placing a ticking clock by your bedside. When you grow drowsy, turn your attention to the clock and go to sleep hearing its ticking say, "I remember better—I remember better."

"Demand good service of your memory," writes William Walker Atkinson, "and it will learn to respond. Learn to trust it, and it will rise to the occasion. How can you expect your memory to give good service when you continually abuse it and tell everyone of 'the wretched memory I have; I can never remember anything'? Your memory is very apt to accept your statements as truth; our mental faculties have an annoying habit of taking us at our word in these matters. Tell your memory what you expect it to do; then trust it and refrain from abusing it and giving it a bad name . . . Our advice is to get acquainted with your memory, and make friends with it. Treat it well and it will serve you well." (45)

(g) *Reintegration*

We remember better if certain conditions present at the time of learning are also present when we try to remember what we have learned. We tend to forget because we try to recall something in circumstances different from those in which we learned it.

When the original conditions of learning are reinstated, remembering is enhanced. This is why it is often helpful when we want to recall something we have forgotten, to retrace our steps and repeat what we were doing when we originally committed the fact to memory.

For example, a man said: "I find that as I lie down in bed I recall a dream of the previous night." He recalled because lying down in bed reinstated the conditions under which he originally experienced the dream.

Again, reintegration occurs when, for instance, we go from one room to fetch something from another room. On arrival there we find that we have forgotten what we went for and in order to remember we have to go back to our starting point and remind ourselves what it was we wanted. Before we can remember we have to reinstate the original conditions under which the resolve to fetch the thing was formed.

This principle is an argument in favour of study taking place each day at the same time. You should sit at the same table or desk in the same room with your books arranged in the same way.

Another application of this principle is that a foreign language should be studied in a setting which resembles as closely as possible that in which it will be used. As Stuart Chase points out in *Guides to Straight Thinking*, words are meaningless unless they can be related to the experience of the speaker and the hearer. (46) This is the basic principle of all language study. From it stems the practical corollary that a foreign language is best learned by living in the country in which it is used. Of course, this is not practicable for all students of foreign languages. In that case the next best thing is to learn in a situation which reproduces as nearly as possible the conditions of the foreign setting.

For example, this is where radio can help; the listener to the BBC series of language broadcasts can overhear French or German voices in a French or German setting, and thus associate directly in his mind the French or German way of saying things with the situation in which they are heard. This is in fact the surest way of learning to speak a language.

(h) *Memory for Completed and Uncompleted Tasks (Zeigarnik Effect)*

Another discovery of practical value is that an uncompleted task is remembered better than a completed one.

"A failure makes one inventive," wrote Freud, "creates a free flow of associations, brings idea after idea, whereas once success is there a certain narrow-mindedness or thick-headedness sets in." (47)

"This is a finding," writes Dr. Robert H. Thouless in *General and Social Psychology*, "which has implications for the practical educator who may reflect on the danger of too early and complete explanation in the process of teaching leaving no tensions to aid remembering." (48)

It means that you should arrange to break off your studies just before you come to the end of a natural division of the subject-matter. If we break off our studies before we have finished a chapter, we shall remember the material better when we return to it later to finish the chapter.

Remembering uncompleted tasks better than completed ones is known as the Zeigarnik effect from the name of the German woman psychologist who discovered it in 1927. It is based on the following experiment.

Subjects were given about twenty tasks, such as modelling

animals, stringing beads and solving puzzles, half of which were allowed to be completed, but the other half were interrupted.

After the experiment the subjects were asked to list all the things they had done. It was found that the uncompleted tasks were remembered much more frequently than the completed ones in spite of the fact that a longer time was generally spent on the completed than on the uncompleted tasks. (49)

Kurt Lewin has attempted a theoretical explanation by postulating that to begin an activity of any kind creates a tension which persists until that activity is finished.

Experiments which have been performed by other psychologists have qualified the results obtained by Zeigarnik. More recent evidence indicates that the Zeigarnik effect applies only to memory for tasks performed without emotional stress. Although people differ widely in this respect, it has been found that, where a person feels that not completing the task threatens his self-esteem, or in other ways places him under emotional stress, the opposite trend occurs. That is to say, when a person is labouring under emotional stress, a completed task is remembered better than an uncompleted one.

The practical application of this principle is that, if you are worried about getting through your work, you will remember what you read better by finishing the chapter than by not finishing it.

In such cases it would seem that the tendency to suppress unpleasant memories is stronger than the Zeigarnik effect, thus making it easier to recall the completed than the uncompleted task.

The Zeigarnik effect is illustrated by the following experience. "I have studied only six lessons," said a student. "I want to complete the course. Unless I can do this I shall continue to have a feeling of something left undone. The unfinished thing is never attractive and I feel it is a nagging wound."

Here is another illustration. A woman went to church when she was too poor to put anything in the collection plate. Soon afterwards she moved away from the neighbourhood and ceased to attend that particular church. But the incident continued to trouble her. Years later, when her circumstances had improved, she sent the rector a cheque for £25 with a note which said that she had felt guilty for many years and wished to make good her omission. This is another example of an uncompleted task being well remembered.

Should failure be associated with a completed task instead of with an uncompleted one, the Zeigarnik effect is reversed. That is to say, the completed task is then remembered better. This is illustrated by the following experiment.

The experimenter told the subject that some tasks were easy and others hard and that he was not concerned about the hard ones. If he saw that the subject was getting along well he would interrupt him, because the experimenter had learned all he needed to know. If the subject was not doing well, the experimenter would let him continue because then he needed to know how long it took to finish the task. Interruption thus became a sign of success and completion a sign of failure. Under these conditions the completed tasks were remembered better than the uncompleted ones. (50)

Atkinson also studied the effect of a person's concern for achievement on his ability to remember completed and un-completed tasks. Three types of test situation were arranged: a relaxed, informal situation; an atmosphere created by the giving of instructions; and a situation in which the testee was urged to do his best, the result being regarded as a measure of intellectual ability, leadership, etc. It was found that more completed tasks were recalled as the atmosphere of the test situation increased from relaxed to ego-involved. This applied also to the un-completed tasks—for persons with a high concern for achievement. However, persons with only a moderate concern for achievement remembered fewer uncompleted tasks as the situation changed from relaxed to tense. In other words, such persons regard their inability to complete a task as a failure which they prefer not to remember, while persons with a high concern for achievement regard the uncompleted tasks as challenges which they remember better in order to be able to complete them. The general conclusion is that we remember uncompleted tasks better when we have the positive goal of attaining success than we do when we have the negative goal of avoiding failure. (51)

Rosenzweig experimented with the solving of jigsaw puzzles by students, who were told that the puzzles were tests of intelligence and had to be completed in a certain time, otherwise they would be removed. Some of the puzzles were allowed to be completed while others were interrupted before they were finished. The students were encouraged to do their best in the available time. It was found that the completed puzzles were remembered better than the uncompleted ones, the former being associated with a sense of achievement, the latter with failure. (52)

An uncompleted task is better remembered than a completed one when a person is interested in the task for its own sake and does not think of success as a boost to his self-esteem or of failure as a threat to it (task-oriented). On the other hand, a completed task is better remembered than an uncompleted one when a person works at it because of what it can do for him, because he regards success as necessary to his self-esteem but is not interested in the work for its own sake (ego-oriented).

This illustrates the fact that material connected with a pleasant feeling is better remembered than that associated with an unpleasant one. Once again we see that memory is not merely a passive process in which material that has been learned fades away with the passage of time. Indeed, as we noted in Chapter 2, Freud explained forgetting as due to an active process of repression which prevents the emergence into consciousness of ideas that are unacceptable to the ego. Our attention is, as it were, turned away from such ideas.

(i) *Figure and Ground* (*von Restorff Effect*)

A thing is remembered better if it contrasts with its background than if it blends with it. If some prankster lets off a firework in the middle of a symphony concert, the audience may remember the explosion better than some passage which occurs in the music. If I see the great white gash of a stone quarry in the Derbyshire hills, I remember this feature of the scene because it stands out from its background of the green countryside.

In the jargon that psychologists are fond of this is known as the *von Restorff effect*. Can it be turned to practical use in the task of learning? The answer is: Yes, it not only can but is so used. For example, when something is put in *italics* in a book, the *italic* print stands out in contrast with its background of roman print. The author uses this device because he wants to call your attention to the importance of the word, phrase or sentence. He hopes that by his so doing you will remember it better.

Even if what is important on a page is not italicised, you can still make it stand out by underlining it. If the book is your own you can do this as you read it and you can refresh your memory by revising the underlined passages.

But the device is also of value in less obvious ways. For example, why do some workers in industry like "music while you work"? The more superficial answer is that it helps to relieve the monotony of their repetitive tasks. Might not an equally valid reason be that the details of the job are remembered better because they contrast with the background of the music?

Is "music while you work" a help to students or merely a hindrance? Some students do indeed report that they can study better to the accompaniment of a background of music. The von Restorff effect explains why this is so. The material for study stands out by contrast against the musical background and may well be remembered better for that reason.

Of course, the musical background mustn't be such as to distract attention from the work. It must remain a background and no more. Therefore, it should for preference be one that is uninterrupted by pauses, without words to the music, and without startling contrasts in the type of music itself. Otherwise it may be more of a hindrance than a help to a person who is trying to study.

A neutral background can be used in the same way in other sense modalities. Why do tea-tasters or wine-tasters rinse their mouths out after each taste? The answer is that they remember the flavour of the tea or wine best if they perceive it against a neutral taste background than if it blends with other tastes still on the tongue.

What about the sense of touch or temperature? If we put a cold hand in hot water the water is remembered as being hotter than if we put the hand in hot water after taking it out of tepid water. Again the hot sensation contrasts more strongly with the cold background than with the tepid one and therefore is remembered better.

The von Restorff effect, then, defines the relationship of figure and ground in terms of the memorability of the former. A thing is remembered better if it contrasts with its background than if it blends with it.

To conclude this section let us remind ourselves again of the practical hints we have discovered for dealing with the second cause of forgetting, i.e. inadequate repetition. They are:

1. *Make sure that you understand what you want to remember.*
2. Study a little and often rather than a lot but seldom.
3. *Recite the material to yourself aloud or silently.*
4. Repeat the material for longer than it takes just to know it.
5. *Learn by wholes rather than by parts.*
6. *Have confidence in your ability to remember.*
7. Conditions like those in which you learned help you to remember.
8. Uncompleted tasks are more easily remembered than completed ones (unless you are afraid of failure or concerned about success, when you may remember a completed task better than an uncompleted one).
9. Something that contrasts with its background is more easily remembered than something which blends with it.

The above principles have been tested and proved in the psychological laboratory. The value of four of them (the ones in italics) was convincingly shown in the following experiment which also illustrated the importance of *concentration* (see pp. 45–58) and of *associations* (see last section of this chapter).

A group of students were given practice for three hours spread over four weeks in memorising poems and nonsense syllables without being told what methods to use. Another group practised memorising poems and nonsense syllables but were instructed in proper methods of memorising. They were taught the use of attention to meaning (comprehension), active self-testing (recitation), learning by wholes, mental alertness (concentration), confidence in one's ability (autosuggestion), and associations (see pp. 85–95). When both groups were given a memory test, the group which had used the above methods averaged 30 per cent to 40 per cent better results than the other. (53)

Are we entitled to assume, as we do in this book, that conclusions reached as a result of experiments conducted in the psychological laboratory are valid when applied to the practical problems of everyday life? This problem itself formed the subject of an experimental investigation carried out in the field of learning by the Russian psychologist D. B. Elkonin.

Elkonin studied an experimental class in which the programme and methods of instruction in the pupils' mother tongue and in arithmetic had been altered in accordance with recommendations based on the findings of experimental research. He found that the amount of time spent in learning the material was reduced and that the quality of the learning was improved. (53a)

3. Avoiding Interference

We now come to the third reason why memories are lost, i.e., through interference from other memories. The practical task that faces us is to discover how such interference can be eliminated or cut down to a minimum.

For a few minutes after a memory trace is formed it is easily disturbed. If left undisturbed the trace hardens or consolidates and can resist interference from other memory traces. During the process of consolidation, however, it is still subject to a type of interference known as retroactive inhibition from later memory traces.

The principle of retroactive inhibition states that the memory trace of an earlier activity is impaired by that of a later one.

In other words, we tend to forget a certain thing not simply because it is a week ago since we learned it, but because we have since learned other things, the memory traces of which have interfered with the memory trace of the original thing.

The problem of memory efficiency, then, is the problem of reducing this interference to a minimum in order to give the memory trace the chance to set or consolidate. The brain begins to forget part of what it has learned almost immediately after learning it. Much of the forgetting occurs during the first fifteen minutes, and is due to the facts being crowded out by new experiences. This means that we must allow something we have learned to set or consolidate in our minds if we are to remember it.

There are several ways in which this can be done.

The most favourable conditions of remembering would occur if no activity at all followed the learning of the material until it had had a chance to become consolidated. The practical application of this principle has been shown by the discovery that if memorising is followed by sleep, the memorised material is retained better than if further waking activity ensues.

We forget less rapidly during sleep than during waking hours. While we are asleep we do not learn other things likely to interfere with the memory of what we have already learned. This fact argues in favour of learning periods being followed by sleep. When we study in the evening we should go to bed afterwards rather than take up further waking activity. This not only helps us to assimilate work already done, but also refreshes us for the work of the following day.

The lesson may be revised in the morning before the activity of the day makes us forget a great deal of it. The process of forgetting is thus delayed not only by the period of sleep but also by the subsequent revision.

Jenkins and Dallenbach have made a special study of this problem. They showed that if subjects retire and sleep immediately after learning, retention after twenty-four hours is better than it is if they remain awake for a few hours after learning. They had their subjects learn certain materials and tested them after one or two or four or eight hours. During these intervals the subjects either slept or were occupied with their normal day's business. The results were invariably superior when the subjects had been sleeping than they were after an equal interval of daytime activities. (54)

Johnson and Swan, too, found that work done just before sleep was 6.5 per cent superior to that performed immediately on waking. (55)

During sound sleep there is, in spite of occasional dreams, probably a minimum of mental activity. Thus we can see why retention is much better during sleep than it is during waking.

Even if we do not sleep after learning, a period of rest or relaxation helps us to remember. If you cannot adopt the above procedure and go to bed after studying, avoid doing any other mental work, especially of a similar kind, before retiring to bed. A few minutes of "taking it easy" directly after learning a lesson make for better remembering than an equal period devoted to strenuous mental activity.

If you must memorise something for use within a short time, try to arrange matters so that the briefest possible period elapses between the time of memorising and the time of recalling. Then the interfering impressions will be as few as possible.

Further strenuous mental occupation, especially of a similar nature, is unfavourable to remembering. The more active we are in the interval, the more likely we are to forget. The greatest loss of retention occurs by shifting directly to material of a very similar kind. However, the better we learn the original task, the more likely we are to remember it even in spite of what we do afterwards.

The greatest loss of retention occurs by shifting directly from one lesson to another of a very similar kind. Therefore the student should see that even if he must engage in further mental activity after learning, it is of as different a kind as possible. If one period of study must be followed immediately by another, arrange to switch to that form of learning which is least similar to the one in which you have just been engaged.

For example, do not follow one branch of mathematics with another, but arithmetic or algebra might very well be followed by a foreign language. After studying psychology one should not turn directly to philosophy but rather to mathematics or chemistry.

There is another way in which mental processes are inhibited, causing us to forget. This is known as the principle of proactive inhibition, which states that mental activity that precedes learning also prevents us from remembering what we have learned. We forget something that we have learned because we have learned other things before. Not merely are old memories obliterated by the new but also new ones by the old.

To illustrate this point with a homely example, we may say that the absent-minded professor leaves his umbrella in the bus not only on account of his wife's reminder to post a letter given to him *after* he picked up his umbrella from the hall-stand, but also on account of the lecture which he prepared the previous night *before* he picked up his umbrella.

Therefore the student would be well advised to see that before commencing to study a lesson he takes a brief rest rather than engaging in other mental activity.

Proactive inhibition also depends on similarity in the same way as does retroactive inhibition. Similarity between the inhibiting and the inhibited processes heightens the degree of the disturbance.

Hence even if you must take up the study of a subject immediately after engaging in some other mental activity, you should endeavour to ensure that it is as different as possible.

All this lends increased plausibility to the theory that forgetting is a matter of disturbing interaction among memory traces rather than of a deterioration which each memory trace undergoes independently (56, 57)

4. REPRESSION

The fourth cause of forgetting is repression. A memory is forgotten by being repressed or denied admittance into the conscious mind. Having something on the tip of one's tongue indicates that a repression is operating; the harder one tries to remember it the more difficult it becomes.

To remember, then, the repression must be relieved. A repressed memory can be recalled if the repression is undone. There are two ways in which this is accomplished. One is by increasing the strength of the memory itself. How to do this has been explained in the three preceding sections of this chapter. The other is by reducing the strength of the resistance opposed to the repressed memory.

For example, if one turns one's attention to other matters, the resistance may be weakened and the repressed memory will pop up spontaneously into consciousness. This is the basis of the method in which we try to recall something by *relying upon the memory occurring to us spontaneously*. A forgotten name may suddenly spring to mind after we cease to think about it.

A name which is "on the tip of your tongue" can be remembered by not trying to remember it. This illustrates the operation of the law of reversed effort, which states that in a conflict between will and imagination the latter proves the stronger. You can use this law in a helpful way by trying not to remember the name (will) but at the same time thinking that you will remember it (imagination). In this conflict imagination proves the stronger with the result that the forgotten name springs to mind.

The recall of material that has temporarily escaped our memory can sometimes be achieved by the simple method of *saying the alphabet* slowly to ourselves, pausing after each letter to allow time for the process of association to work. If the forgotten material is framed in words, sooner or later we must come to a letter which is associated with one of those words. The association may lead to the recall of the forgotten material in its entirety. As soon as we utter the letter in question, what we are seeking to remember may occur to us. For example, a housewife said: "I remembered a name by going through the letters of the alphabet."

A man said: "I have quite a number of photographs of my war-time army comrades mounted in an album. The name of the person is written on the back of the photograph. Having forgotten most of the names, I decided to try a little experiment to remember them. I just thought of the person for a few minutes and then mentally went through the alphabet, and on reaching the initial letter of the wanted name, I found that the name itself followed. When a name came to mind, it proved, on looking at the back of the photograph, to be right. This is the method I have always used for remembering names and have found it very successful."

This method can be adapted to recalling foreign language equivalents of English words. The English word should be held in mind and the foreign alphabet worked through until the equivalent is remembered.

It can also serve if the material is in algebraic form, e.g. an algebraic equation. If the material is wholly in numerical form, try *saying numbers to yourself*, starting with 0. In this way you may be able to recall forgotten telephone numbers, house numbers, dates, sums of money, football and cricket scores, etc.

The resistance to a repressed memory also becomes weaker in sleep, so that during a dream we may recall something which has been repressed in waking life. Therefore the memory can be recalled by *interpreting a dream*. This is a problem which the author has dealt with in two previous books to which the reader is referred for further information.*

Sometimes we can recall something forgotten by *being reminded of it through something said or done* during the course of the day. For example, a lady said: "If I cannot remember a name or

* *Dreams, Their Meaning and Significance* (Thorsons, 1956) and *The Right Way to Interpret Your Dreams* (Elliot Right Way Books, 1961).

address, I leave it at the back of my mind for an hour or so and continue with my work; then quite suddenly something will happen to remind me of it."

Another method useful for recalling memory material is "sleeping on it." This is described as follows by a person who tried it. "I have my own system," she said, "for recalling forgotten material. On retiring I tell myself silently that I shall recall what I want to know, and then I promptly go to sleep. I wake up in the morning nearly always knowing the answer to my problem."

(a) *The Solution of Problems in Sleep*

Another instance is that of a university student who said: "Whilst asleep I solved a mathematical problem which had defeated me when awake. Every week-end I have mathematical problems to work out. I am in the habit of working on them on Saturday evenings. One evening, however, I couldn't fathom a certain problem. Nor could I do so on Sunday, but went to bed on Sunday night and worked it out in a dream. On Monday I found that I was the only one who had been able to solve it out of a class of over fifty."

Inspiration often comes in this way. For example, a schoolboy would go to sleep with problems still unsolved. As he awoke in the morning the answers were quickly obtained.

In *From the Workshop of Discoveries*, O. Loewi writes as follows (58):

"In the night of Easter Saturday, 1921, I awoke, turned on the light, and jotted down a few notes on a tiny slip of paper. Then I fell asleep again. It occurred to me at six o'clock in the morning that during the night I had written down something most important, but I was unable to decipher the scrawl. That Sunday was the most desperate day in my whole scientific life. During the next night, however, I awoke again, at three o'clock, and I remembered what it was.

"This time I did not take any risk; I got up immediately, went to the laboratory, made the experiment on the frog's heart . . . and at five o'clock, the chemical transmission of nervous impulse was conclusively proved."

Sometimes one comes across a case in which a person seems to remember something which he has never experienced. In a way inspiration itself is rather like this. Nevertheless, such an explanation is probably more apparent than real. Here is an instance in which a person recalled something he had no recollection of ever having experienced.

A doctor said that he once heard an elderly patient who was delirious speaking fluent French, although normally the patient knew nothing of the language. Let us assume that the patient had served in France in World War I. The French he would hear would be recorded in an odd corner of his unconscious mind, from which it might well emerge in delirium. Perhaps the patient was not in France in World War I? Very well, then—he had been to France since? He had heard French people speaking in this country? He had seen a French film? Any one of a number of possibilities might account for his knowledge of that language. Somehow or other the man must have come into contact with spoken French, and this experience lay at the root of his behaviour in delirium.

Reintegration (see pages 68–69) can also be used as a method of recalling something which has been temporarily repressed or forgotten. This is illustrated by the following experiences reported by Miss C. L.:

"As a child at school and on other occasions I was often told, when asked a question, 'You won't find the answer on the ceiling!' But the point was that I *did*. For example, I would be asked, 'What was the date of the Battle of Hastings?' If I was in the same room I had only to look at the same object which I had been watching when told the date. Then it would come back to my mind in a flash."

The forgotten memory may be recalled even if the attendant circumstances are only reinstated in imagination instead of in reality. As the above person put it:

"If I was in another room I would use the ceiling to project a mental picture of the scene where I learned the date, and then the answer would be there. I still do this, especially with music. For example, I can recall the title of a tune which is running through my head by thinking of the instrument on which I first heard it played."

"Some years ago," she went on, "I used to work in a neighbour-hood where there are a number of small streets whose names I didn't know. I always managed not to lose myself until one evening on my way home from work I stopped and realised I must have taken a wrong turning somewhere. I found my way by going back to a spot I remembered and starting off again from there."

She hoped that reinstating the original conditions under which she learned the route would enable her to recall the memory of it.

Therefore, if you are trying to bring something back to mind, *repeat or imagine yourself repeating the situation in which you originally experienced it.*

(b) *Free Association*

Usually, however, a special technique is required to relieve a repression. The best method of weakening the resistance is, in fact, the method known as "free association."

Free association has been described by Freud as putting oneself "into a condition of calm self-observation, without trying to think of anything, and then to communicate everything which he becomes inwardly aware of, feelings, thoughts, remembrances, in the order in which they arise in his mind." A person doing this should avoid any inclination "to select from or to exclude any of the ideas (associations), whether because they are too 'disagree-able,' or too 'indiscreet' to be mentioned, or too 'unimportant' or 'irrelevant' or 'nonsensical' to be worth saying . . . he has only to attend to what is on the surface consciously in his mind, and to abandon all objections to whatever he finds, no matter what form they take." (59)

To make practical use of this method get a pencil and a writing pad; retire to some quiet place; think of something connected with what you want to recall, and ask yourself: "What do I remember next?" Write down whatever comes to mind. Then ask yourself again: "What do I remember next?" Again write the answer. Proceed thus until you recall the desired memory or until you have had enough and put the method aside for the next sitting.

A simple example of a chain of associations that resulted in the recall of a forgotten name is given by Freud in his *Introductory Lectures on Psycho-Analysis* (p. 92). He found that he could not remember the name of the small country on the Riviera of which Monte Carlo is the capital. "I delved into all my knowledge about the country; I thought of Prince Albert . . . of his marriages, of his passion for deep-sea exploration—in fact of everything I could summon up, but all to no purpose. So I gave up trying . . . and, instead . . . let substitute names come into my mind . . .; Monte Carlo . . . Piedmont, Albania, Montevideo, Colico . . . Montenegro . . . Then I noticed that four of the substitute names have the same syllable 'mon,' and immediately I recalled the forgotten word . . . 'Monaco'." (60)

He adds the reason that led him to forget the name for the time being: "Monaco is the Italian name for Munich, and it was some thoughts connected with this town which had acted as an inhibition." This illustrates the third or fourth of the causes of forgetting mentioned on page 33, i.e., interference from other impressions or the repression of an unpleasant memory.

Another example will be found in Theodor Reik's *The Inner Experience of a Psycho-Analyst*, where the author tells how by means of free association of ideas he remembered the poem in which occur the lines, "for when true love awakens, dies The Self, that despot, dark and vain." (61)

Use of the above method has evoked some encouraging reports from persons who have tried it. For example, one of them said: "I have tried the free association of ideas exercise with great success. It usually takes only about five or ten minutes to recall a name, which in some instances arrives suddenly 'out of the blue' after a relaxation of effort."

Another reports: "I have practised the memory exercise of free association of ideas, and find that I really can remember names and data from years previous."

"I thought about the person whose name I wished to recall and as many things about him as I could remember," said a woman, "and I was then able to recall the name."

Recently the writer was unable to remember the address of a relative who lived in a town in Hertfordshire. He applied the simple method prescribed above. Writing down all the ideas that the name of the town reminded him of, he very soon arrived at the address he was seeking.

"It worked, taking about twenty minutes," said a man. "I

started with a crotchet sign used in music, went on to 'tune,' then 'Tunley,' and finally 'Nunley,' which was the name I wanted."

"I tried it," said a Nigerian student, "and remembered a name which in my language is the word for rolling a piece of wood on the ground. It is 'Abiri.' In calling the name to mind I saw a mental image of a man rolling a piece of wood on the floor."

A young woman said: "I tried to remember the name of my German teacher at school. Amongst other things, woods, trees and flowers kept cropping up. The German for tree is Baum and the teacher's name was Baumgarten."

"There were huge gaps in my memory," stated a man. "I have relived several past experiences and have gone back in memory through a great part of my childhood days by means of free association of ideas. My memory is now complete." This result was achieved in less than five months.

"I have been doing the free association of ideas," said Mr. N. V., "and I now realise how the unconscious mind speaks in a language of symbols. On trying to remember the name of a friend whom I knew in the Services, I ended with a mental picture of a park with lots of sun. The chap's name is Parkinson."

The author wanted to recall the name of a man with whom he had had some dealings. He remembered that the man lived in Wales. He therefore sat down and asked himself: "What does Wales remind me of?" He wrote down the name "Mason." Then he asked himself: "What does Mason remind me of?" He wrote "home." He continued to practise this simple method for a few minutes, writing down the following chain of associated names: Jones—Carless—Curtis—Clapham—King—Royal—Roy—Ray—Raines—Real—Simpson—Smart—Trevor—Cannon—Walters. The next name that came was recognised as the one sought: Williams.

A student said: "I tried free association of ideas for remembering the meaning of the French word *coudrier*. I didn't go on very long before I got as far as 'willow tree.' Then I thought of 'green.' I connected 'green' with 'hazel twigs,' so I got it in the end. *Coudrier* means 'hazel tree.'"

"I find," said Mrs. R. D., "that I have been using very much the same method as this for calling things to mind all my life. I tried the experiment with the story of *Jane Eyre*, which I read at ten years of age. It was possible to recall the whole story."

Mr. L. E. said: "I tried to recall the name of my maths master at school. I thought of old school pals, escapades, dreams and hopes, school exercises. Whilst browsing among these memories of the past, I recalled being given a lift in his car. Then I remembered his name: Mr. Carson!"

(c) *Laws of Association*

The principle of association is invaluable not only in relieving repressions, but also in memorising the material we wish to retain.

For example, do you have difficulty in remembering whether to write *separate* or *seperate*? To separate means to part. Associate *separate* with *part*, and you will easily remember the spelling.

In church you go up for communion to the altar rail and it is important that on your return you should find the right pew. Since they all look alike how are you to do it? You can associate the position of your pew with something else, e.g. you can remind yourself that it is three rows behind the churchwarden's pew, or that it is level with the third column from the foot of the chancel steps, etc.

According to the press, a security firm who provide a bandit-proof safe rely upon the principle of association. They arrange that only the proprietor of the safe shall know the combination which opens it, and they instruct him to remember it by associating it with something personal to himself, such as a birthday, wedding anniversary, etc.

Association of ideas is a basic fact of mental life which has been known since the days of Aristotle. It accounts for the way in which one idea occurs after another. For example, on the day when a woman was moving out of a house, she had a mental "flashback" to the day, twenty-one years before, when she had moved into it. The "flashback" occurred because the present experience was associated with the earlier one.

Another illustration is given by a teacher who said: "During my training I learned, in teaching something new, to tag it on to something the children already knew."

There are three laws of association (similarity, contrast, contiguity). The law of association by similarity states that two ideas may be associated if they resemble each other. For example, trying to remember a name, a man thought of a pigeon, then of a pouter pigeon. Then the name came to him: Poulter. It was associated with "pouter" by similarity.

In another instance the name Ede, which a man had been trying to recall for several days, was associated by similarity with Sir Anthony Eden. The name flashed across his mind when he picked up an evening newspaper and started to read an article about the former Prime Minister.

A third case which illustrates the law of association by similarity is the following. A woman reported: "I tried to remember a name. I had a session of writing down my memories, but without result. Then I left it, but, on thinking about it afterwards, this thought came into my mind, 'What a *hue* and cry all over a name!' The missing name was *Hughes*."

The law of association by contrast states that two ideas may be associated if they contrast with each other. For example, someone mentions the word "day." We at once think of the word "night."

The law of association by contiguity states that two ideas may be associated if they have occurred together. For example, a well-known song has the line: "Moonlight and roses bring memories of you." Moonlight and roses were associated by contiguity with the song writer's beloved because they had probably all been present together on the same occasion.

Vergilius Ferm in an article on "Memorising" in *A Dictionary of Pastoral Psychology* says that he remembers 1859 as the date of the publication of Darwin's *Origin of Species* because he associates it with the year preceding the founding of his alma mater in 1860. (62) This, too, illustrates the law of association by contiguity.

Another illustration is provided by a man who said: "On holiday some years ago I met a man who was a home decorator by trade. We became good friends and he offered to decorate my home very cheaply at any time. When I wanted to take advantage of his services, I was unfortunately unable to remember his name. I wrote down all I remembered about his appearance and character, but with no success. But at a second sitting, while trying to recall any other ideas associated with him, I thought of the fact that he was willing to do a *job* for my family; then I recalled his name. It was *Work*."

Ideas are more likely to be associated the more frequently, recently and vividly they have occurred together. The laws of frequency (or repetition), recency and vividness (or intensity) are known as the secondary laws of association, in contrast to the ones already mentioned, which are known as the primary laws of association.

The law of frequency states that two things are more likely to be associated the more frequently they have occurred together. Frequently performed acts, habits or responses tend to be learned better than those infrequently practised. For example, a student said: "The more I study my lesson the more I understand it." Reliance upon the drill method of instruction exemplifies the use of this principle of learning, which emphasises the number of repetitions employed during the learning period.

The law of recency states that two things are more likely to be associated the more recently they have occurred together. For example, it is a common experience to find that the dreams we remember deal with the events of the day before.

Suppose two sides of an argument, e.g., in a debate, are presented to an audience in succession. Which will be remembered better—the one presented first or the one presented last? Is it better to "get your oar in first" or to "have the last word"?

This question has been settled by an experimental study in which the subjects listened to recorded broadcasts of news items. The items were presented in a different order to each of twelve groups of subjects. After hearing the broadcasts the subjects were tested to find out which items they remembered best.

It was found that the items in the second half of the broadcast were remembered better than those in the first half. The conclusion we are entitled to draw is that from the point of view of memory it is better to have the last say. (63)

The law of intensity or vividness states that two things are more likely to be associated the more vividly they have occurred together. This principle holds that the more vivid an impression is, the better it is retained.

For example, a housewife stated: "The dreams that I remember for a long time afterwards are much more distinct than the ones I remember only for the next morning." Or, as Mr. E. P. C. put it:

"My recollections of a dream are dependent upon the vividness of the dream."

The law of frequency raises an interesting problem. This is the question of whether repetition in itself is sufficient to ensure that something is learnt or that a skill is acquired. The common belief that it is is enshrined in the popular saying that "Practice makes perfect." How far is this supported by modern psychological theory? If I work at a subject long enough, can I be sure that in time I shall master it?

Discussing this question, a writer remarks, "Mere frequency of repetition is now known to play only a minor part in learning. Effective motivation is necessary for learning to take place. An enormous number of repetitions made passively without the intention to learn are proved to be ineffective compared with a much smaller number made with effort to retain the learned material."

Another writer quotes the case of the subject of an experiment in a psychological laboratory who was supposed to memorise a list of nonsense syllables. After the list had been passed before him many times without his giving the signal that he was ready to recite, the experimenter remarked that he seemed to be having trouble in memorising the syllables. "Oh! I didn't understand that I was to learn them," he said, and it was found that he had made almost no progress. The will to learn, in fact, was absent.

In another experiment the subjects tried to draw three-inch lines while blindfolded. They practised drawing hundreds of lines, but were not told how well they were doing. As a result they showed no improvement. As soon as the psychologist began to say, "Right," when they succeeded, the subjects began to improve. This experiment illustrates that mere repetition by itself does not ensure that a skill is acquired. (64)

Psychology thus proves the fallacy of the popular axiom that "Practice makes perfect" by showing that incessant practice without effective motivation or the intention to learn does not make perfect. Without a strong reason for doing an act, it merely makes a moderate level of skill more automatic. Motivation is an important factor in learning and acquiring a skill.

To the above three main laws of association the American psychologist Thorndike added a fourth, which is known as the law of assimilation or the principle of generalisation. This states that a person may react towards a whole situation as he has reacted towards some part of it or towards the whole or part of some other situation like it.

This is illustrated by the curious phenomenon of memory called *déjà vu*, to which reference has already been made in Chapter 2 (see page 39). The explanation we advanced there was that the present situation seems familiar because it resembles in part or in whole some situation in the past which we have now forgotten. We react with the feeling that "we have been here before" towards the situation because we have already reacted in that way towards some part of it or towards some situation like it.

Again, a person may react towards all of a group of people as he has reacted towards some or one of them. Someone who has repeatedly experienced defeat or failure in one situation or a few may come to experience feelings of inferiority in a large number of situations. As the proverb puts it, "Once bitten, twice shy."

For example, a girl said: "In my childhood, if my mother took offence at something I had chanced to say, she would not speak to me for days or even weeks on end. Now I am afraid to say anything to other people in case I should offend them." She was reacting to other people as she had learned to react to one person in her childhood.

By association, then, is meant the tendency to link impressions with other impressions already in the mind or acquired at the same time or place. Everyone appreciates the value of association as a means of recalling faces and events of the past which have been apparently quite obliterated. Every idea that we have is associated with other ideas, and by following back the lines of association a distinct image can be reproduced.

We should *take advantage of all rational associations of ideas* to improve our memorising. The more impressions there are associated with the thing to be remembered, the readier and more certain is its recollection. It is as if there are several paths converging into one. It is only necessary to find any one of these paths and follow it to reach the desired goal. The obvious conclusion is that the greater the stock of knowledge possessed by a mind the easier it is for that stock to be augmented.

(d) *How to Use Association*

Suppose your wife gives you a letter to post. What can you do to ensure that you remember to post it? The answer is: associate the letter with the idea of the first letter-box you see. Then when you actually see the letter-box, you will recall the need to post the letter. The sight of the letter-box will bring the letter to your mind.

Again, a resemblance between an incident in history and a current event may form an association that will enable the event in history to be easily recalled.

In the learning of foreign language words the principle of association is especially useful.

Two Russian psychologists conducted an experiment in which German words new to the secondary school pupils being tested were translated without explanation. This method was compared with that in which the translation was accompanied by an etymological explanation of the word's meaning. They found, as might be expected, that words memorised by the second method were retained better and longer than the "one-word" translation method. (64a) The reason is that the second method has two great advantages:

1. It enables the learner to form stable associations between words he already knows in his own or the foreign language and the new word he wishes to learn.
2. Working out the etymological connections is a more active method. It makes the pupils think more, demanding more of them and stimulating their intellectual activity better than the passive method of committing to memory the German word and its meaning.

Let us take a simple example to illustrate this point. Suppose you want to learn the German equivalent for "boy." To do this by the first method would mean that you study the following one-word translation:

der Knabe—boy

To present vocabulary in this form is the method adopted almost uniformly in language textbooks. Can we wonder that language teaching rarely achieves the results that are expected of it?

Let us compare this method with the second method, in which

the one-word translation is supplemented by an etymological explanation. The material to be learned might then be presented as follows:

> der Knabe—boy (The German word *Knabe* is cognate with the English word "knave," which originally meant "boy" but now has a pejorative sense.)

The inclusion of this explanation means that between *der Knabe* and "boy" we insert an associative link which makes remembering easier. In reality the way we are now presenting the material is like this:

$$der\ Knabe— \frac{\text{associative link}}{\text{(knave)}} —boy$$

Furthermore, by setting ourselves the task of digging out this piece of etymological information we have played a more active part in memorisation than is required by the simple act of trying to learn the one-word equivalent. *To take a more active part in learning is a help in remembering the material better.*

All learning is, in fact, governed by this fundamental principle of associating one thing with another. You can make use of it by discovering the relations between the various parts of what you are studying and by linking up what you learn with what you know already.

For example, in the army a recruit is taught to remember fire orders by associating them with the letters of the word D R I N K. Thus he is taught to associate D with Designation, R with Range, I with Indication, N with Number of rounds, and K with Kind of fire.

Another familiar example is the rhyme that associates the months with the number of days in each. We are able to remember how many days each month has by recalling "Thirty days hath September, April, June and November . . ."

A child learning the piano is taught to remember the names of the notes in the spaces of the treble clef by associating them with each other in the word F A C E. Similarly, the notes on the lines in the treble clef are remembered by associating them with the initial letters of the words in the sentence "*E*very *G*ood *B*oy *D*eserves *F*un."

The present writer, who had studied Latin before he took up German, remembers the order of adverbs in a German sentence by associating the initial letters of Time, Mode and Place with their order in the Latin word T E M P U S.

A useful mnemonic for remembering the seven deadly sins is P E L A G A S—Pride, Envy, Lust, Anger, Gluttony, Avarice, Sloth.

A more elaborate one for remembering the names of English counties is: "Three Boys and three Men from the London and North Western Civil Defence Headquarters at YORK took their GCE in six Subjects." This sentence gives all forty-three counties of England, including the Channel Islands and the Isle of Man. It works out as follows:

Three B(oys): Bedfordshire (1), Berkshire (2), Buckinghamshire (3).

Three M(en): Middlesex (4), Monmouthshire (5), Isle of Man (6).

The word "quarters" in "Headquarters" gives you a clue that for each of the letters L, N, W, C, D and H there are four counties:

L(ondon): Lancashire (7), Leicestershire (8), Lincolnshire (9), London (10).

N(orth): Norfolk (11), Northamptonshire (12), Northumberland (13), Nottinghamshire (14).

W(estern): Warwickshire (15), Westmorland (16), Wiltshire (17), Worcestershire (18).

C(ivil): Cambridgeshire (19), Cheshire (20), Cornwall (21), Cumberland (22).

D(efence): Derbyshire (23), Devonshire (24), Dorset (25), Durham (26).

H(eadquarters): Hampshire (27), Herefordshire (28), Hertfordshire (29), Huntingdonshire (30).

The word "YORK" gives us four more: Yorkshire (31), Oxford (32), Rutland (33), Kent (34).

From GCE we get: Gloucestershire (35), Channel Islands (36), Essex (37).

And the remaining six are given by:

Six S(ubjects): Shropshire (38), Somerset (39), Staffordshire (40), Suffolk (41), Surrey (42), Sussex (43).

(e) *How to Remember a Speech*

A man had to propose the toast of the bridegroom's parents at his daughter's wedding reception. He wanted to know how he could remember his speech.

The speech was as follows:

Ladies and Gentlemen, —

In proposing this toast I must ask you to overlook my inexperience as a public speaker. I hope that what I have to say will atone for any shortcominges in the way I say it.

I would like to take this opportunity of thanking Mr. and Mrs. ——————— for the son they have given my wife and me, and I hope that they will think that the daughter we have been happy to give them is a fair "swop." I would like to improve upon the old maxim that "a trouble shared is a trouble halved" by saying that a happiness shared is a happiness doubled.

——————'s parents may well be proud of their son to-day, for they see him taking the first step on a new and rewarding path. That this step is being taken in company with our daughter is a cause of rejoicing and thankfulness to my wife and myself.

We all hope that the lucky couple will be inspired by the example of harmony that they see in the marriage of Mr. and Mrs. ———————. I am sure that you all share with me the hope that the latter, too, will be able to look back on this day as one of the happiest in *their* lives.

It was not my intention to make a long speech, and already I am overrunning the time I allowed myself. Let me conclude, then, by asking you to rise and drink the health of Mr. and Mrs. ———————.

The man who was to propose the above toast said: "I have always had a shocking memory for anything learned by heart. At school I was never able to remember anything, even though I had tried very hard and had spent a long time over it. Sometimes, after a great deal of effort, I can memorise a short piece, but when I have to speak it before other people it runs out of my brain like water through a sieve."

To anyone else with the same difficulty we offer the same suggestion as to this man. If you want to remember a speech, the thing to do is to make use of a mnemonic. As we have seen, this is a device employing the principle of association. In the case of a speech it is a key word which we can associate with the contents of the speech. All you have to do is to remember the key word, which will remind you of what you want to say.

The above speech consists of five paragraphs, which can be remembered with the help of the mnemonic word UTTER. Each letter of this word gives a clue to the contents of one paragraph. For example, the first paragraph deals with the speaker being *unused* (U) to public speaking; the second paragraph is an expression of *thanks* (T); the third paragraph deals with *taking* a step *together* (T); the fourth paragraph refers to the *example* (E) set by the bridegroom's parents; and the fifth paragraph is a *request* to the company to *rise* (R).

By means of this simple application of the principle of association the whole speech can be committed to memory.

In *Effective Speech* (65), D. E. Watkins and H. F. de Bower recommend that the outline of a speech on personality can be remembered by associating it with the sentence "Fellows Succeed Exceptionally who Consider Personality." The first letter of each of the main words in this sentence is the first letter of a word denoting a quality of personality. Thus F stands for Friendship, S for Sympathy, E for Earnestness, C for Conscience, and P for Physical well-being.

Here is another example of the use of association in remembering. Do you have trouble remembering how to alter your clock when British Summer Time begins and ends? Do you put it forward in spring and back in autumn, or back in spring and forward in autumn? The correct method can be remembered by associating it with two little phrases with which you are already familiar: "Spring forward—fall back." The word "fall," of course, means "autumn."

Students in teachers' training colleges are taught that an essential stage in preparing their lessons is to ask themselves what the pupils already know about the subject they intend to teach. This is so that they can build on sure foundations, associating the new with the old. It is yet another illustration of the value of association in training the memory.

Now let us summarise what we have learned in the form of four practical hints:

1. Give your full attention to what you wish to remember.
2. Repeat it until you know it really well.
3. Make yourself more interested by means of autosuggestion.
4. Take advantage of associations of ideas.

Attention—Repetition—Interest—Association: these are the keys to a better memory.

CHAPTER 4

HOW TO FORGET

No discussion on how to remember would be complete without some reference to how to forget. It will be the purpose of the present chapter to make good this omission.

Indeed to some unhappy and disappointed people forgetting may be more important than remembering. They may have undergone upsetting experiences which they would prefer to put behind them but do not seem able to do.

"Memory has its important and proportionate place in the scale of mental life," writes Dr. Henry Knight Miller in an essay on "The Ministry of Forgetfulness" (*Life Triumphant*, p. 137). "So has 'forgettery.' We need to learn the fine art of relegating into the mental discard life's sordidness, griefs, errors, failures and disappointments. . . . The capacity to forget is an essential pre-requisite for happiness. You cannot be happy while constantly pursued by haunting memories of past transgressions, errors and failures." (66)

Just as it is possible to deduce practical hints on remembering from knowing what causes forgetting, the same information can yield us practical help in forgetting what we wish not to remember.

The type of experience which people would like to be able to forget is illustrated by the following report: "I was a cook in a firm's canteen. A group of employees presented a petition to the manageress that the meals were not satisfactory. This was a great shock to me. I had received no complaints direct. The humiliation is for ever tormenting me. Can you tell me how to forget this unpleasant memory?"

What we have learned about the causes of forgetting may be briefly summarised as follows:

1. We forget because the experience makes a weak impression.
2. We forget because of the lapse of time.

3. We forget because we did or thought something else afterwards or beforehand.
4. We forget because we repress certain memories.

1. WEAK IMPRESSION

The first principle is that we forget because the impression is a weak one. Often, of course, the experiences that prove difficult to forget do so for the very reason that they have left a strong impression. They are often experiences that have been strongly charged with unpleasant emotions. But even experiences of this kind can be weakened in their effect, if dealt with at the time when they occur.

We have seen that when an experience occurs it leaves a physical trace in the brain structure. This physical trace takes a certain time to "settle" before it becomes firmly embedded in the mind. During this process of "consolidation," as it is called, the memory trace is subject to interference and may even be erased completely.

If the experience is denied this settling-down period by the immediate introduction of fresh experiences, it fails to consolidate or to make a proper impression. The result is that its effect upon the mind is considerably reduced.

"You can only recall an impression," writes Dr. Miller, "when you are attending to it. If you refuse to attend to it as it knocks at the door of consciousness and demands attention, it will be relegated, temporarily at least, into the realm of forgetfulness."

Bergson suggested that the function of the brain and nervous system is in the main eliminative—to protect us from being overwhelmed and confused by shutting out most of what we should otherwise remember at any moment, and leaving only what is likely to be useful.

It may be that the time required for the brain to consolidate memories serves this eliminative function. At any rate, for a few minutes after a memory trace is formed it is easily disturbed; if left undisturbed it "hardens" or consolidates and can resist interference.

We shall have more to say about this topic and its practical application to the problem of forgetting under the heading of "Interference" later on in this chapter.

2. Disuse

The second principle is that we forget because of the lapse of time. The fact that an impression has consolidated does not mean that it will not fade eventually. Although this natural process of forgetting is slow and passive, it can still be useful to the person who wishes to erase an unpleasant memory.

It means, in fact, that such a person has time on his side. For example, a man said: "I saw the body of a man who had been knocked down and killed in a road accident. The thought of this incident has kept on coming back to my mind in spite of my efforts to forget it. I want to get rid of this unwanted memory, although I am pleased to say that *it is somewhat decreasing day by day*."

"As we look back over the years," reflects Dr. Miller, "the friendly hand of time tends to place in proper perspective those experiences which, when we were passing through them, seemed unbearable. Now they add just a touch of colour to the picture life paints and are needed to give the proper and complete background."

3. Interference

Nevertheless, one should not rely purely and simply upon the passing of the years to mend a broken heart. Besides the slow and passive method one should make use of a quick and active method. The difference between the two may be likened to a wound which is left undressed and one which receives medical attention. The healing power of nature will clear up the former in time. But the latter will heal more promptly and cleanly.

We have seen that it is not so much time itself that counts as the use that we make of it. Of course, the two are really inseparable, since no one can live in a mental or social vacuum, nor have experiences without growing older. We should, however, seek other experiences which will help us to forget the unpleasant experience. The effectiveness of this remedy depends upon four conditions:

(a) *The greater the similarity of needs involved in the unpleasant experience and what we do or think afterwards, the easier we shall forget the former.* For example, the best cure for a broken love affair is a new one that is successful. Try moving around a bit, and see what it does for you. There are plenty of people with whom you can fall in love and satisfy your emotional needs.

(b) *The more active we are in the interval, the more likely we are to forget.* This means that the more impressions we can superimpose on an unpleasant one, the better our chances of forgetting it. It underlines the value of keeping yourself busy after you have undergone something that has upset you.

When something happens which you want to forget, lose no time in obliterating it with other impressions. Don't seclude yourself and brood over the event. Don't fall a victim to feeling sorry for yourself. Resist the inclination to indulge in self-pity. Instead, get out and do things. Get among new people, and see new faces, new scenes. Avoid going to the places which in your mind are associated with the broken romance. A change of environment is what the doctor orders in such a situation.

(c) *The less vivid the effect of the original impression, the less likely are we to remember it and the more will other activities help us still further to forget it.* Of course, this is not always easy to arrange. We cannot always control the intensity of the disappointing experiences that we undergo. However, where we can it is as well to do so.

(d) *There is more forgetting during waking activity than during sleep.* For example, suppose you came home one evening and found a letter from your beloved telling you that she intended to marry another man. If you decided to sleep on the problem, you would give the memory a better chance to consolidate than if you went out and saw an exciting film.

The further waking activity of watching the film would help you to forget your disappointment better than if you went to bed and slept, and much better than if you went to bed and lay awake turning the problem over and over in your mind.

Of course, this is something which is easier to preach than to practise. You have to weigh up, however, the pros and cons of the matter. You have to put in the balance the trouble of making yourself do something active against the chance of forgetting something which, unless forgotten, will make you miserable.

We also forget an event because of what we did or thought *before* it happened. This is an argument in favour of doing or thinking at all times positive and constructive things which will form a kind of mental reserve pool upon which we can draw for consolation in time of need or distress. The man or woman who in later years can look back upon a life of solid achievement, having contributed something to the world, can stand unshaken when the tempests of vicissitude rage around him. To be able to feel that one may have left the world just a little better for his having lived in it is bound to provide a source of strength buttressing one against the rude shocks of existence.

4. REPRESSION

Although repression has no practical application to the problem of how to forget, there is a closely allied mental process which has the advantages of repression without its disadvantages. Some people have the knack of being able to push an undesirable memory to the back of their minds. Although they think about it occasionally, it does not keep on forcing itself on their attention. This is known as suppression. For those who are capable of it suppression offers a practical way of disposing of an unwanted memory—at least temporarily.

The teaching of psychology has sufficiently emphasised the evil effects of repression, which is responsible for the production of much mental and bodily sickness of various kinds. Suppression, therefore, should not be confused with repression. Whereas repression means that one refuses to acknowledge a thought or memory, suppression amounts to acknowledging and controlling it, because by so doing a person realises that he will favour his chances of eventual happiness and success.

When we suppress we are aware both of what we are suppressing and of the fact that we are suppressing; in repression, on the other hand, we are no longer aware of what is repressed, nor are we aware of the process by which we do the repressing.

To summarise, then, we can encourage the forgetting of an unpleasant experience if we:

1. Introduce fresh experiences which prevent the unwanted memory from "settling down."
2. Rely upon the healing power of time.
3. Satisfy in another way the need which the unpleasant memory has frustrated.
4. Seek fresh interests or a change of environment.
5. Remember that waking activity helps us to forget better than "sleeping on it."
6. Build up throughout life a reserve stock of pleasant experiences upon which we can look back when things go against us.
7. Push the unpleasant experience to the back of our minds.

CHAPTER 5

SUMMARY OF PRACTICAL HINTS ON REMEMBERING AND FORGETTING

1. WHAT IS MEMORY?

REMEMBERING is the activity of attending to present ideas which are determined by past experiences. A past event which we are able to revive as a present experience leaves a physiological change in the brain structure called a memory trace.

Pure memory is the activity of attending to a particular experience, as, for example, when I remember what I ate for my Christmas dinner last year. Habit memory is the knowledge acquired by experience as distinct from the particular experiences of acquiring it.

Memory differs from both imagination and thinking. The function of images in memory is to represent past experiences. In imagination the images relate to what is thought of as occurring in the future. Past experience is made use of both in memory and in thinking, but whereas memory is a direct use of what has been learned, thinking is an indirect use. Remembering is performing a previously learned act, while thinking is doing something partly original.

2. WHY DO WE FORGET?

You read and reread a chapter in a book, yet a few minutes afterwards you cannot relate one word of what you have read. This is usually caused by lack of attention, so that the experience does not make a proper impression upon us.

Forgetting is also due to the lapse of time between an experience and the attempt to recall it. As a result of the normal metabolic processes of the brain a memory trace tends to fade or decay with the passage of time, unless we renew it by repeating the experience which gave rise to it. Much of what we learn is forgotten almost as soon as we have learned it. Forgetting proceeds most rapidly immediately after learning but less rapidly as the interval increases.

Changes occurring in the brain with the passing of time also lead to things being "remembered" that never occurred or that occurred differently from the way they are remembered. (Distortion)

The view that the lapse of time alone accounts for the decay of a memory trace is too simple. For a few minutes after a memory trace is formed it is easily disturbed. If left undisturbed, the trace hardens or consolidates and can resist interference. During the process of consolidation, however, the memory trace is still susceptible to a type of interference known as retroactive inhibition from material which is learned subsequently (and also, as we shall see later, from material which has been learned before).

This has led to the formulation of the view that we forget because we do or think something else afterwards. The principle of retroactive inhibition states that the trace left behind by an earlier activity is impaired by a later one.

This means that we tend to forget a certain thing not simply because it is a week ago since we learned it, but because we have since learned other things the memory traces of which have interfered with the memory trace of the original thing. The more active we are in the interval, the more likely we are to forget. The better we learn the original task, the more likely we are to remember it in spite of interpolated activities.

As we noted in Chapter 3, there are certain conditions under which retroactive inhibition operates. One of these is that the greatest loss of retention occurs by shifting directly to material of a very similar kind. The more a later experience resembles an earlier one, the more likely are we to forget the latter. But a point is eventually reached when the similarity is close enough to assist the remembering of the original material rather than interfere with it.

If waking activity interferes with recall, we should remember better after sleep, when less activity has intervened. You do, in fact, forget less when asleep than when awake. You lose a little during the first hour or two of sleep, but after that you forget very little more during the night. For example, a person who read a story before going to sleep could remember many details when he was awakened. When he remained awake after reading the story, he forgot more of the details.

The principle of proactive inhibition states that work which *precedes* learning also tends to interfere with the retention of the learned material. What happened before an experience causes us to forget it as well as what happened afterwards.

There is also a process of unconscious forgetting of painful memories known as repression. Such memories may not be recalled because of the sense of anxiety or guilt which they would provoke if they were. We tend to remember events which give us satisfaction and to forget those which are annoying to us. We more easily forget an experience which conflicts with our comfort and self-esteem than one which does not. The tendency of a memory to become repressed varies directly with the anguish which accompanies it.

Senility, too, is a cause of forgetting, although as it cannot be eliminated we are not concerned with it in this book. Some people approaching old age can barely remember the events of the day, although their memory for events of the distant past and child-hood may be unimpaired. This type of forgetting occurs through the organic changes taking place in the brain and nervous system with the passing years.

A poor memory is caused, then, by the memory trace not having much energy to begin with, by not being recharged or fading with the lapse of time, and by losing its energy to other memory traces. There is also a form of forgetting, known as repression, caused by resistance or opposition from something else in the mind to the recall of a painful memory.

The main causes of forgetting may thus be briefly summarised as follows:

1. We forget an experience because it makes a weak impression on us.
2. We forget an experience because we don't refresh our memory of it.
3. We forget an experience because other experiences interfere with it.
4. We forget an experience because it creates a conflict between the wish to remember it and the wish not to remember it.

3. How Can We Remember?

The first cause of a poor memory is that an experience makes a weak impression on us. To secure a strong impression it is necessary to concentrate on what we wish to remember.

Lack of concentration is caused by the habit of day-dreaming, lack of interest in the subject, too little or too much muscular tension, and worry or emotional conflict, which distracts attention from what we are doing.

Therefore, we can acquire the habit of concentration if we:

1. Bring our mind back every time it wanders to other things.
2. Strengthen our interest in the subject by means of auto-suggestion.
3. Lightly brace ourselves (but not too much) as we work.
4. Try to deal with the emotional problems that distract our attention.

The second cause is that we allow time to elapse without refreshing our memory. This cause can be removed by repeating whatever it is we wish to remember. The more frequently a thing is repeated, the more likely it is to be remembered.

To be most effective in refreshing our memory repetition depends upon certain conditions, which may be stated in the form of the following practical rules:

1. Always make an effort to understand the material which you are repeating.
2. A few minutes' repetition every day is better than a greater amount of repetition less often.
3. A better method of repetition than reading and rereading is to read and then try to recall what has been read.
4. Do not repeat what you wish to remember until you barely know it, but until you know it really well.
5. It is better to repeat the material as a whole than to break it up into parts and repeat each part separately.
6. Use autosuggestion to acquire confidence in your ability to remember what you repeat.
7. Repeat your work at the same table or desk in the same room with your books arranged in the same way.
8. Break off your repetition before you come to a natural

division of the subject-matter, for if you are working without emotional stress you will remember an uncompleted task better than a completed one. On the other hand, if you are more interested in what the study can do for you than in the study itself, it may be better to complete the task, for you will remember a completed task better than an uncompleted one.

9. Try to arrange that what you wish to learn contrasts in some way with the background against which you are studying it.

The third cause of forgetting is that the memory traces of other experiences interfere with the memory trace of the experience we wish to remember. This interference is less active during sleep than during waking hours. It is less active between different types of material than between similar types. It concerns what we do before an experience as well as what we do afterwards.

The practical application of these principles to the problem of overcoming retroactive and proactive inhibition is as follows:

1. Go to bed after studying in the evening rather than take up further waking activity.
2. Revise the material in the morning before the activity of the day makes you forget too much of it.
3. Avoid other mental work, especially of a similar kind, in the event that you cannot go to bed after studying.
4. Change to a different form of learning in the event that one period of study must be followed by another.
5. Take a brief rest before studying a lesson rather than engage in other mental activity, especially similar mental activity.
6. Endeavour to ensure that it is a different type of study if one period of study must be immediately followed by another.

The fourth cause of forgetting is repression. There are various ways in which a repression can be undone, thus helping us to remember better.

1. We can rely upon the repressed memory occurring to us spontaneously.
2. We can run through the alphabet until we come to a letter associated with the repressed memory.
3. We can run through consecutive numbers, starting with 0,

until we come to one which reminds us of the forgotten number.

4. We can recall a repressed thought or memory by interpreting a dream which embodies it.

5. We can wait to be reminded of the repressed memory by some happening during the course of the day.

6. We can often remember something by "sleeping on it." If we take a problem to bed with us, we may find that in the morning we remember how to solve it.

7. We can repeat or imagine ourselves repeating the situation in which we first experienced what we want to recall.

8. We can make use of free association, writing down whatever thoughts occur to us until we recall the repressed memory.

9. We should also make use of any available associations in committing something to memory. Two ideas may be associated if they resemble or contrast with each other, or if they simply occur together.

4. How Can We Forget?

A study of the four causes of forgetting yields practical hints on how to forget as well as on how to remember. These practical hints may be briefly summarised as follows:

1. Weaken the impression left by a disturbing emotional experience by turning your attention to fresh experiences as soon as possible after it has occurred.

2. Rely upon the power of time to heal the wounds of the soul. The person who wishes to forget an unpleasant experience has time on his side.

3. Find other interests that will help to obliterate the disappointments of the past. Seek other experiences that will erase the memory of the previous unpleasant experience. The greater the similarity of needs involved, the easier we shall forget the disappointment. The best cure for a broken love affair is a new one that is successful.

Keep yourself busy after you have undergone something likely to upset you. Avoid going to the places which in your mind are associated with the broken romance. Don't go to bed and sleep immediately after a disappointing experience, but get out and get a change of scene to take your mind off the problem.

4. Build up throughout life a reserve stock of pleasant experiences upon which you can look back when things go against you.

5. Avoid expecting to banish unpleasant memories by "repressing" them, i.e., by denying to yourself that they ever occurred. This method of forgetting has no practical application to the problem, because it is not under the conscious control of the will but occurs without our being aware of it, and because unless what is repressed is sublimated or worked off indirectly, it leads to the appearance of nervous symptoms. But what you shouldn't repress you may be able to suppress. That is, you may be able to push it more or less to the back of your mind so that it is not bothering you all the time.

"Refresh Your Memory" Quiz

Check each statement by ringing True *or* False *in pencil*

1. Past experiences are determined by present ideas. True/False
2. Past events leave a memory trace in the brain. True/False
3. Pure memory means attending to a particular past experience. True/False
4. Habit memory is the knowledge acquired by experience. True/False
5. Past experiences are represented in memory by images. True/False
6. An experience makes a weak impression on us unless we attend to it properly. True/False
7. A memory trace is normally strengthened by the passage of time. True/False
8. Little of what we learn is forgotten as soon as we have learned it. True/False
9. When we "remember" things that never occurred this is called "distortion." True/False
10. The lapse of time alone accounts for the decay of a memory trace. True/False
11. If left undisturbed a trace hardens or consolidates. True/False
12. Doing or thinking something else afterwards does not make us forget. True/False
13. The better we learn something the less we are likely to forget it. True/False
14. The more a later experience resembles an earlier one, the more likely are we to forget the latter. True/False
15. What we learn is forgotten faster while we are asleep than while we are awake. True/False
16. A topic swotted up before going to bed stays in our mind the following morning. True/False
17. Work which precedes learning tends to interfere with the remembering of learned material. True/False

18. The forgetting of pleasant memories is known as repression. TRUE/FALSE

19. Something which conflicts with our self-esteem is forgotten slower than something which doesn't. TRUE/FALSE

20. Senility is never a cause of forgetting. TRUE/FALSE

21. Organic changes take place in the brain as we grow older. TRUE/FALSE

22. We get a strong impression of what we wish to remember if we concentrate on it. TRUE/FALSE

23. Lack of concentration is caused by day-dreaming. TRUE/FALSE

24. We can concentrate on a subject better if we are not interested in it. TRUE/FALSE

25. Too little or too much muscular tension causes lack of concentration. TRUE/FALSE

26. Worry distracts our attention from what we are doing. TRUE/FALSE

27. Autosuggestion can be used to strengthen our interest in a subject. TRUE/FALSE

28. To concentrate better we should tense ourselves strongly as we work. TRUE/FALSE

29. We should repeat whatever we wish to remember. TRUE/FALSE

30. The less often it is repeated the better it is remembered. TRUE/FALSE

31. The better you understand something the better you can remember it. TRUE/FALSE

32. "Lots but seldom" is a better study rule than "little but often." TRUE/FALSE

33. Reading and rereading is the best method of study. TRUE/FALSE

34. Something you wish to remember should be repeated only until you barely know it. TRUE/FALSE

35. It is better to repeat your material as a whole than to break it up into parts. TRUE/FALSE

36. Confidence in your ability to remember can be acquired by means of autosuggestion. TRUE/FALSE

37. It is better to move about from room to room than always to study in the same place. TRUE/FALSE

38. When we are working under emotional stress an uncompleted task is remembered better than a completed one.   TRUE/FALSE

39. An item which blends with its background is better remembered than one which contrasts with it.   TRUE/FALSE

40. Other memory traces do not interfere with the memory trace we wish to remember.   TRUE/FALSE

41. It is better to take up further waking activity than to go to bed after studying in the evening.   TRUE/FALSE

42. The material we have learned in the evening should be revised the following morning.   TRUE/FALSE

43. If one study period is immediately followed by another it should if possible be a different subject.   TRUE/FALSE

44. A repressed memory can occur to us spontaneously.   TRUE/FALSE

45. A repressed memory can be recalled by interpreting a dream.   TRUE/FALSE

46. A problem can be solved by "sleeping on it."   TRUE/FALSE

47. Free association means writing down whatever thoughts come into our head.   TRUE/FALSE

48. Two ideas may be associated if they resemble each other.   TRUE/FALSE

49. Two ideas may be associated if they contrast with each other.   TRUE/FALSE

50. Two ideas may be associated if they have occurred together.   TRUE/FALSE

51. To take a more active part in learning is a help in remembering.   TRUE/FALSE

52. To forget turn your attention to fresh experiences.   TRUE/FALSE

53. We can rely upon the power of time to help us to forget.   TRUE/FALSE

54. The best cure for a broken love affair is a new successful one.   TRUE/FALSE

55. A reserve stock of unpleasant experiences is a source of comfort in troubled times.   TRUE/FALSE

56. Repression is under the conscious control of
    our will.   TRUE/FALSE
57. Repression is a cause of nervous symptoms.   TRUE/FALSE
58. Suppression means pushing something to the
    back of your mind.   TRUE/FALSE

KEY TO "REFRESH YOUR MEMORY" QUIZ

1, 7, 8, 10, 12, 15, 18, 19, 20, 24, 28, 30, 32, 33, 34, 37, 38, 39,
40, 41, 55 and 56 are FALSE; the rest are TRUE. The above items
should read as follows:

1. Present ideas are determined by past experiences.

7. A memory trace is normally weakened by the passage of time.

8. Much of what we learn is forgotten as soon as we have
   learned it.

10. The lapse of time alone does not account for the decay of
    a memory trace.

12. Doing or thinking something else afterwards makes us forget.

15. What we learn is forgotten slower while we are asleep than
    while we are awake.

18. The forgetting of unpleasant memories is known as repression.

19. Something which conflicts with our self-esteem is forgotten
    faster than something which doesn't.

20. Senility is a cause of forgetting of recent events.

24. We can concentrate on a subject better if we are interested
    in it.

28. To concentrate better we should not tense ourselves too much
    as we work.

30. The more often it is repeated the better it is remembered.

32. "Little but often" is a better study rule than "lots but
    seldom."

33. Reading and rereading is not the best method of study; a
    better method is to read and then try to recall what has
    been read.

34. Something you wish to remember should be repeated until
    you know it really well.

37. It is better to study in the same place than to move about from room to room.

38. When we are working under emotional stress a completed task is remembered better than an uncompleted one; OR When we are working without emotional stress an uncompleted task is remembered better than a completed one.

39. An item which contrasts with its background is better remembered than one which blends with it.

40. Other memory traces interfere with the memory trace we wish to remember.

41. It is better to go to bed after studying in the evening than to take up further waking activity.

55. A reserve stock of pleasant experiences is a source of comfort in troubled times.

56. Repression is not under the conscious control of the will.

Appendix

HOW TO READ FASTER

WHAT is read and understood quickly is remembered at least as well as what is read and understood slowly and may be remembered better. With quicker reading, says Harry Bayley, "the amount of the material which is remembered after one reading is at least as much, and generally more, than that remembered after a slow reading. . . . You can read twice as fast and remember just as much." Discussing the view that better understanding comes from reading more slowly and carefully, he comments that this is "Excellent advice for the beginner, but an impediment to the efficient." (67)

The average reader can read between two hundred and three hundred words per minute. A slow reader reads between a hundred and two hundred words per minute, while a fast reader may read up to four hundred words per minute.

In reading a line the eyes make several jumps. This is because they are reading separate words or phrases. A fast reader makes three or four jumps per line on the average. This means that he reads three or four words at a time. A slow reader may make a dozen or more jumps. This is because he reads each word separately and looks back at words already read.

To train yourself to read faster you should practise making fewer eye movements. Fix your eyes on the centre of each line, and then let them run down the page instead of across it. Try not to say the words to yourself, and don't look back at what you have already read. Begin with simple material such as short stories and other light literature. As your reading rate improves, choose more difficult material.

"Improved speed in my reading," said Mr. R. D., "came to me when I timed myself on short articles, essays and other such brief items. The sense of speeding up was quickly acquired and easily carried over from the shorter work to book-length reading."

If you want to, you can cut a slit in a postcard wide enough and high enough to expose one full line at a time. By sliding it down the page as you read you can force yourself to read at a faster pace. This idea is adapted from a training film in which a few words are illuminated at a time, beginning at 180 words per minute and working up to 570 words per minute.

To aid this practice of fast reading two psychologists, Dr. Goodwin Watson and Dr. Theodore Newcomb, have formulated five simple rules.

1. Eliminate whispering, pointing and movements of the lips, head and hands as you read. Such movements tend to slow up your reading and distract the mind from its effort to understand what you read.
2. Practise relaxation of your muscles. Sit down to read in an easy-chair. Make sure that you are physically comfortable.
3. Try to read phrases, sentences, or even paragraphs rather than single words.
4. Try not to let your mind wander. If you find yourself thinking of something else, write down a note about it to be taken up later. See pages 45–58 of this book about how to concentrate.
5. Try to anticipate the argument the author is setting forth. Ask yourself whether he is developing his ideas on the lines you would expect.

Get a general idea of what you are going to read before you begin to read it. You can learn quite a lot about a book from the dust-jacket and from reviews published in newspapers and literary periodicals. The table of contents, the preface, the author's own summaries of his arguments, and the index also give a lot of information. One can get the hang of the subject by mastering the headings and subheadings. If you want to get a firm grasp of a book's contents in the least possible time, you can obtain help from all these sources.

Do not attempt to read too much all at once at the increased rate. If you keep on for a long time, fatigue will tend to set in and you will revert to your slower rate of reading. That is why short practice periods are desirable at the start. When the faster rate becomes habitual, however, it is no more tiring than a slower rate.

"My eyes are centred the middle word in each line," said a man who followed this method of reading, "and instead of moving from left to right, they travel straight down the centre of the page, taking in a line at a time. I learned to do it when I was a student, and it saves me hours every week spent on reading."

Understanding is, of course, just as important as speed. It may be asked what sense there is in reading fast if a person does not understand what he reads. The answer is that it is better to read what one does not understand rapidly than to read it slowly. The sooner one discovers that one does not understand it, the sooner one can go over it again or go on to some other book that explains it better.

Therefore, to see whether you have gathered ideas and information from rapid reading, it is as well to close the book from time to time and jot down what you have read or run over it in your mind. Read for five or ten minutes and then stop to think about what you have read. If something the author has said has confused you or seems contrary to fact, go back and read the passage over again, thinking about the doubtful point.

A student said: "My experience is that speedier reading is reading with greater understanding because you have to keep alert to maintain the speed and this wide-awakeness means more attention to the subject-matter. I find that I take away practically as much from a speedy reading as from a leisurely one."

A book can also be read rapidly by "skimming" through it. If you know what not to read, you can pick out the more important parts, just casting your eye over the less important ones. Some things need plenty of concentration, while others call for less of it. It is wise to adjust your method to the material. Learn the art of judicious skipping. Discriminate between what is and what is not worth your attention.

Theodore Roosevelt was once lent a book by a diplomat at a reception. At the close of the evening he handed the book back with a brief comment. The diplomat was offended because he thought that the President had not read the book. Roosevelt thereupon led him to his study, where he discussed the book's contents with him. The President was a rapid reader and had slipped away from his guests to master the book.

Learning more words also helps one to read faster. "By constantly reading," said Mrs. B. G., "I have become much more familiar with words and their meanings. Having a better knowledge of words, I can read with greater speed than before."

Pay attention, too, to your eyesight. Have your eyes tested and, if necessary, have glasses fitted. Defects of sight are obstacles to rapid reading. Be sure that there is enough light but avoid glare on the page. Once the eyes become tired reading is slower and poorer.

If you want to put into effect the recommendations offered above, first of all measure your normal reading speed. You can do this by timing yourself as you read the following passage, which contains two hundred words. Read at the comfortable rate which you adopt every day, being careful to take in the meaning of what you read.

Start timing yourself now. To remember a thing it is necessary to pay attention to it. Much impaired memory is really impaired concentration. We do not remember a thing because our attention is distracted from it by something else. Besides repeating it and so establishing it firmly it is necessary to be interested in it. Remembering it is also assisted if we associate or link it up in the mind with something which is already there. The conditions upon which association depends are: similarity, contrast and contiguity. We can associate two things if they resemble each other. For example, we can associate the Italian word *tutto* with the French word *tout*. We can associate by contrast. An English motorist who takes his car to the Continent remembers to drive on the right side of the road by contrast with the left side on which he drives in England. Association also occurs by contiguity. Two things may be associated with each other because they have occurred together in space, e.g., apples and custard, or time, e.g., Christmas and carols, or both, e.g., Hiroshima and the atomic bomb. These four points— Attention, Repetition, Interest and Association—may be remembered by means of the mnemonic word A R I A. *Stop timing yourself now.*

You can work out your normal reading speed from the following table:

Time in seconds	*Reading speed in words per minute*
80	150
75	160
70	171
65	185
60	200
55	218
50	240
45	267
40	300
35	343

If your reading speed is not shown above you can work it out by dividing 12,000 by the number of seconds you took to read the piece.

Now read the following passage, which contains one hundred words. This time read as fast as you can without loss of comprehension. Deliberately force yourself to read at a faster pace than you normally do. Again time yourself.

Start timing yourself now. Most people in reading fixate their attention on the left of the page and let the eyes (sometimes the head as well) move across to the right. To speed up your rate fix your attention on the centre of the page and let the eyes move downwards, taking in a line at a time. Comprehension improves as speed improves, or it can be improved separately. This is done by reading a section and then, having closed the book, asking yourself questions about it, running over it in your mind, discussing it with someone else, or answering written questions about it. *Stop timing yourself now.*

Now check your new reading speed from the following table. If it is not shown divide 6,000 by the number of seconds you took.

Time in seconds	Reading speed in words per minute
35	171
32	188
30	200
28	214
25	240
23	261
20	300
18	333
15	400
12	500
10	600

This experiment will give you some idea of how with a little effort you can quicken up your speed of reading. What is needed now is regular practice for a few minutes each day to make your new reading speed habitual.

Are these methods of any value when put into practice? Let the results speak for themselves. For example, a group of banking and industrial employees registered approximately 275 words per minute to begin with. After ten weeks this tempo was increased to 450 words per minute, and the actual comprehension was increased from 45 to 70 per cent of the matter read.

A group of U.S.A.F. officers increased their reading speed from 292 words per minute to 488 words per minute after six weeks; the slowest officer stepped up his own pace from 106 words per minute to 226 words per minute, and the fastest increased it from 456 words per minute to 810 words per minute.

The question of whether reading speed can be improved without loss of comprehension has been tested experimentally with results which confirm that it can. John Morton of the University of Reading investigated the value of a commercial reading efficiency course. He tested G.P.O. executives, whose ages ranged from twenty-one to sixty-three, before, immediately after and at least six months after the course. He found that their speed of reading was increased but that they understood just as well when they read faster. The mean improvement in reading speed immediately after the course was 64.9 per cent, and even after six months it was still 39.5 per cent. (68)

Paraphrasing Bacon's famous quotation "Reading maketh a full man," we may say that "fast reading makes an efficient man."

REFERENCES

(The author gratefully acknowledges his debt to the authors and publishers of the works cited in this bibliography.)

1. Dunlop, Erwin. You and your memory. *Psychology*, 1954, 18, No. 3.
2. Roback, A. A. *History of American Psychology*. New York: Library Publishers, 1952, pp. 365, 362.
3. Heimann, Paula. Certain functions of introjection and projection in early infancy. In Klein, Heimann, Isaacs and Riviere. *Developments in Psycho-analysis*. London: Hogarth Press, 1952, p. 147.
4. Ellson, D. G. Hallucinations produced by sensory conditioning. *Journal of Experimental Psychology*, 1951, 28, 1–20.
5. Miller, Henry Knight. *Practical Psychology*. Marple: Psychology Magazine, 1961, p. 79.
6. Ebbinghaus, H. *Memory*. New York: Columbia University Teachers College, 1913.
7. Gilliland, A. R. The rate of forgetting. *Journal of Educational Psychology*, 1948, 39, 19–26.
8. Freud, Sigmund. *Moses and Monotheism*. London: Hogarth Press, 1939.
9. Meltzer, H. Individual differences in forgetting pleasant and unpleasant experiences. *Journal of Educational Psychology*, 1930, 21, 399–409.
10. McGranahan, D. V. A critical and experimental study of repression. *Journal of Abnormal and Social Psychology*, 1940, 35, 212–225.
11. Diven, K. Certain determinants in the conditioning of anxiety reactions. *Journal of Psychology*, 1937, 3, 291–308. Cited in Lundin, Robert W. *Personality: An Experimental Approach*. New York: Macmillan, 1961, pp. 276–277.
12. Blum, G. S. *Psychoanalytic Theories of Personality*. New York: McGraw-Hill, 1953.
13. Zeller, A. F. An experimental analogue of repression. I. Historical summary. *Psychol. Bulletin*, 1950, 47, 39–51.
14. Taylor, Charles, and Combs, Arthur W. Self-acceptance and adjustment. *Journal of Consulting Psychology*, 1952, 16, 89–91. Reprinted in Dulany, DeValois, Beardslee and Winterbottom. *Contributions to Modern Psychology*. New York: Oxford University Press, 1958, pp. 269–273.

15. Thompson, George G. and Witryol, Sam L. Adult recall of unpleasant experiences during three periods of childhood. *Journal of Genetic Psychology*, 1948, 72, 111–123.

16. Allport, G. W. *Personality: A Psychological Interpretation.* New York: Holt, 1937.

17. Freud, Sigmund. Leonardo da Vinci and a memory of his childhood. *Standard Edition.* London: Hogarth Press, Vol. XI, pp. 84–85.

18. Freud, Sigmund. *Psychopathology of Everyday Life.* London: Benn, 1948, Part XII.

19. Desmond, Shaw. *Reincarnation for Everyman.* London: Rider, 1950.

20. Freud, Sigmund. *Op. cit.* Part X.

21. Jacobsen, E. *Progressive Relaxation.* Chicago: University of Chicago Press, 1938.

22. Courts, F. A. Relations between experimentally induced muscular tension and memorization. *Journal of Experimental Psychology*, 1939, 25, 235–256. Cited in Hilgard, Ernest R. *Introduction to Psychology.* London: Methuen, 1957, p. 11.

23. Freud, Sigmund. *Inhibitions, Symptoms and Anxiety.* London: Hogarth Press, 1936, p. 77.

24. Wiksell, Wesley. The relationship between reading difficulties and psychological adjustment. *Journal of Educational Research*, 1948, 41, 557–558.

25. Mursell, James L. *Streamline Your Mind.* London: Watts, 1954.

26. Cantril, H., and Allport, G. W. *The Psychology of Radio.* New York: Harper, 1935, pp. 196–200. Quoted in Abelson, Herbert I. *Persuasion.* London: Crosby Lockwood, 1960, p. 47.

27. Ebbinghaus, H. *Op. cit.*

28. Miller, Henry Knight. *Op. cit.*

29. Katona, G. *Organizing and Memorizing.* New York: Columbia University Press, 1940, pp. 188–189.

30. Ebbinghaus, H. *Op. cit.*

31. Fraser, John Munro. *Psychology.* London: Pitman, 1951, p. 147.

32. Aveling, Francis. *Directing Mental Energy.* London, p. 94.

33. Lorge, I. Influence of regularly interpolated time intervals on subsequent learning. *Teachers' College Contributions to Education*, No. 438.

34. Snoddy, G. S. Evidence for a universal shock factor in learning. *Journal of Experimental Psychology*, 1945, 35, 403–417.

35. Gates, A. I. Recitation as a factor in memorizing. *Archives of Psychology*, 1917, 7, No. 40.

36. Hovland, C. I., Lumsdaine, A. A., and Sheffield, F. D. *Experiments*

on Mass Communication. Princeton University Press, 1949, pp. 288 ff. Quoted in Hovland, C. I., Janis, I. L., and Kelley, H. H. *Communication and Persuasion.* Yale University Press, 1963, p. 217.

37. Forlano, G. School learning with various methods of practice and rewards. *Teachers' College Contributions to Education,* 1936, No. 688.

38. Seibert, L. C. A series of experiments on the learning of French vocabulary. *Johns Hopkins University Studies in Education,* 1932, No. 18.

39. Dainow, Morley. *Personal Psychology.* London: Pitman, 1935, p. 103.

40. Krueger, W. C. F. The effect of overlearning on retention. *Journal of Experimental Psychology,* 1929, 12, 71–78.

41. Krueger, W. C. F. Further studies in overlearning. *Journal of Experimental Psychology,* 1930, 13, 152–163.

42. Seibert, L. C. *Op. cit.*

43. Keller, F. S. Studies in international morse code. I. A new method of teaching code reception. *Journal of Applied Psychology,* 1943, 27, 407–415.

44. Fisher, S., and Cleveland, S. E. *Body Image and Personality.* New York: Van Nostrand, 1958, p. 9.

45. Atkinson, William Walker. *Your Mind and How to Use It.* Holyoke, Mass.: The Elizabeth Towne Co.; London: Fowler, 1911, pp. 59–61.

46. Chase, Stuart. *Guides to Straight Thinking.* London: Phoenix House, 1959, p. 34.

47. Freud, Sigmund. Letter to Martha Bernays, Oct. 31, 1883.

48. Thouless, Robert H. *General and Social Psychology.* London: University Tutorial Press, 1937, p. 52.

49. Zeigarnik, B. Das Behalten erledigter und unerledigter Handlungen. *Psychol. Forsch.,* 1927, 9, 1–85.

50. Marrow, A. J. Goal tensions and recall. *Journal of General Psychology,* 1938, 19, 3–35, 37–64.

51. Atkinson, J. W. *The Projective Measurement of Achievement Motivation.* Unpublished Ph.D. thesis, University of Michigan, 1950. In McClelland, David C. *Groups, Leadership, and Men.* Pittsburgh: Carnegie Press, 1951. Cited in Dulany, DeValois, Beardslee and Winterbottom. *Contributions to Modern Psychology.* New York: Oxford University Press, 1958, p. 225.

2. Rosenzweig, S. Need-persistive and ego-defensive reactions to frustration as demonstrated by an experiment on repression. *Psychological Review,* 1941, 48, 347–349. Cited in Lundin,

Robert W. *Personality: An Experimental Approach*. New York: Macmillan, 1961, p. 315.

53. Woodrow, H. The effect of type of training upon transference. *Journal of Educational Psychology*, 1927, 18, 199–172. See Woodworth and Schlosberg, p. 746.

53a. Elkonin, D. B. A psychological investigation in an experimental class. *Voprosy Psikhologii*, 1960, 5, 29–40.

54. Jenkins, J. G., and Dallenbach, K. M. Oblivescence during sleep and waking. *American Journal of Psychology*, 1924, 35, 605–612.

55. Johnson, H. M., and Swan, T. H. Sleep. *Psychological Bulletin*, 1930, 27.

56. Robinson, E. S. Some factors determining the degree of retroactive inhibition. *The Psychological Monographs*, 1920, 28, No. 6.

57. Whitely, P. L. The dependence of learning and recall upon prior intellectual activities. *Journal of Experimental Psychology*, 1927, 10, 489–508.

58. Loewi, O. *From the Workshop of Discoveries*. University of Kansas Press, 1953.

59. Freud, Sigmund. *Introductory Lectures on Psycho-analysis*. London: Allen & Unwin, 1929, pp. 242–243.

60. Freud, Sigmund. *Op. cit.*, p. 92.

61. Reik, Theodor. *The Inner Experience of a Psycho-analyst*. London: Allen & Unwin, 1949.

62. Ferm, Vergilius. Memorising. In Ferm, Vergilius. *A Dictionary of Pastoral Psychology*. New York: Philosophical Library, 1955, p. 143.

63. Tannenbaum, P. H. Effect of serial position on recall of radio news stories. *J. Quart.*, 1954, 31, 319–323. Quoted in Abelson, Herbert I. *Persuasion*. London: Crosby Lockwood, 1960, pp. 6–7.

64. Thorndike, E. L. *The Fundamentals of Learning*. New York: Columbia University Teachers College, 1932.

64a. Krasilshchikova, D. I., and Khokhlachev, E. A. Memorization of foreign words as affected both by the mode of explaining their meaning and by memorization time. *Voprosy Psikhologii*, 1960, 6, 65–74.

65. Watkins, D. E., and de Bower, H. F. *Effective Speech*. Marple: Psychology Publishing Co.

66. Miller, Henry Knight. The ministry of forgetfulness. In *Life Triumphant*. Marple: Psychology Magazine, p. 137.

67. Bayley, Harry. *Quicker Reading*. London: Pitman, pp. 2, 183, 19.

68. Morton, John. An investigation into the effects of an adult reading efficiency course. *Occupational Psychology*, 1959, Vol. 33, No. 4, pp. 222–237.

SOME OTHER BOOKS ON MEMORY

Allen, C.: *Passing Examinations: A Psychological Study of Learning, Remembering and Examination Techniques* (H. K. Lewis, 1963).

Ballard, P. B.: *Obliviscence and Reminiscence* (British Journal of Psychology Monograph Supplement) (Cambridge University Press).

Bartlett, F. C.: *Remembering* (Cambridge University Press).

Bayley, Harry: *Quicker Reading* (Pitman).

Bornstein, Arthur: *Bornstein's Miracle Memory Course* (Prentice-Hall, 1964).

Brothers, Joyce: 10 *Days to a Successful Memory* (Prentice-Hall).

Bugelski, B. R.: *The Psychology of Learning* (Holt, 1956).

Bullas, A.: *Lycéens, vous pouvez acquérir une mémoire extraordinaire* (Editions J. Oliven).

de Saint Laurent, Raymond: *Memory* (Aubanel Publishers).

Ebbinghaus, H.: *Memory* (Columbia University Teachers College, 1913).

Fidlow, Michael: *How to Strengthen Your Memory* (Foulsham, 1962).

Flesch, Rudolf, Witty, Paul, *et al.*: *How You Can Be a Better Student* (Mayflower).

Freud, Sigmund: *Psychopathology of Everyday Life* (Penguin Books).

Froe, Otis D., and Lee, Maurice A.: *How to Become a Successful Student* (Wilshire).

Furst, Bruno: *The Practical Way to a Better Memory* (Grosset & Dunlap, 1944; Fawcett Publications, Inc., 1957; Psychology Publishing Co. Ltd., 1962).

— *Stop Forgetting* (Doubleday, Garden City Books, 1960; Memory and Concentration Studies, 1962).

Furst, Bruno, and Furst, Lotte: *You* Can *Remember!* (Memory and Concentration Studies).

Glendening, P. J. T.: *Teach Yourself to Learn a Language* (English Universities Press, 1965).

Hopkins, Francis G.: *How to Understand and Train Memory* (Hopkins, 1964).

Hunt, H. Ernest: *How to Train the Memory* (Foulsham).

Hunter, Ian M. L.: *Memory: Facts and Fallacies* (Penguin Books).

Katona, G.: *Organizing and Memorizing* (Columbia University Press).

Kelvin, R. P.: *Advertising and Human Memory* (Business Publications, 1962).

Laird, Donald A., and Laird, Eleanor C.: *Techniques for Efficient Remembering* (McGraw-Hill).

Leedy, Paul D.: *Reading Improvement for Adults* (McGraw-Hill).

Lewis, Norman: *How to Read Better and Faster* (Thomas Y. Crowell Co.).

Logan, Arthur L.: *Remembering Made Easy* (Arco Publications Ltd.).

Lorayne, Harry: *How to Develop a Super-power Memory* (Thomas).

Mace, C. A.: *The Psychology of Study* (Penguin Books, 1962).

Maddox, Harry: *How to Study* (Pan Books, 1963).

McGeoch, J. A.: *The Psychology of Human Learning* (Longmans, Green, 1942).

Meredith, Patrick: *Learning, Remembering and Knowing* (English Universities Press, 1961).

Morgan, C. L.: *How to Study* (McGraw-Hill, 1962).

Niblett, W. R., ed.: *How and Why do we Learn?* (Faber, 1965).

Orton, J. Louis: *Memory Efficiency and How to Obtain It* (Thorsons).

Pear, T. H.: *Remembering and Forgetting* (Methuen).

Pettit, Lincoln: *How to Study and Take Exams* (Rider).

Philp, Howard L.: *Memory: How to Make the Most of It* (The Psychologist Magazine).

Pitkin, Walter B.: *The Art of Rapid Reading* (The Psychologist Magazine).

Poppelbaum, H.: *Memory and Its Cultivation* (New Knowledge Books).

Rapaport, D.: *Emotions and Memory* (International Universities Press).

Smith, Nila Banton: *Be a Better Reader* (Prentice-Hall).

Starrett, Robert S., and Powers, Melvin: *A Practical Guide to Better Concentration* (Wilshire, 1962).

Strong, Alan: *Pass That Exam!* (Thomas, 1963).

Tocquet, Robert: *Cultivez votre cerveau: volonté, attention, mémoire* (Editions Les Productions de Paris).

Travers, Robert M. W.: *The Essentials of Learning* (Collier-Macmillan. 1963).

Weinland, James D.: *How to Improve Your Memory* (Barnes & Noble).

Wood, E. E.: *Mind and Memory Training* (Pitman).

Young, Morris N.: *Bibliography of Memory* (Chilton Company, 1961).

INDEX

action theory, 54
active method, 91
advertising, direct-mail, 26
amnesia, infantile, 33
  reasons for, 33
  senile, 31, 38, 104
Aristotle, 85
assimilation, law of, 89
association, laws of, 85–89, 107
  value of, 89
  how to use, 90–92
Atkinson, J. W., 71
Atkinson, W. W., 68
attention, 45–48
  active and passive, 57–58
  definition of, 24, 46
  law of, 24, 48, 55
  value of, 48
audiles, 20
autosuggestion, 51, 59, 67, 105
Aveling, Francis, 62

belongingness, law of, 60
Bergson, H. L., 97
Berlioz, H., 28
Blum, G. S., 30

Chase, Stuart, 69
Combs, A. W., 30
comprehension, 59–61, 105
concentration, 45–57, 105
  summary of advice on, 57, 105
confabulation, 39
confidence, 67–68
consolidation, 27, 75, 97, 103
contiguity, 86
contrast, 86
Courts, F. A., 54

Dallenbach, K. M., 76
day-dreams, 48

de Bower, H. F., 94
déjà vu, 39–44, 89
  definition of, 39–40
  examples of, 39–44
  explanations of, 41–44
  in dreams, 43–44
Desmond, Shaw, 41
Dickens, Charles, 40
Dictionary of Pastoral Psychology,
  A, 86
distortion, 103
disuse, 23, 25–27, 98
Dreams, Their Meaning and Significance, 79

early memories, 35–38
Ebbinghaus, H., 25, 26, 60, 61
Effective Speech, 94
ego-orientation, 72
eidetic image, 18
Elkonin, D. B., 75
emotional conflict, 55–57

"faculty" psychology, 14
fantasy, 38
  unconscious, 43
Ferm, Vergilius, 86
Field, Shirley Ann, 36
figure and ground, 72
forget, how to, 96–101, 107
  summary of hints on, 101, 107–
  108
forgetting, causes of, 23–44, 45,
  96–97, 102–104
  summary of practical hints on,
  107–108
  rate of, 25, 102–103
  and sleep, 76, 99, 103
free association, 82–85, 107
  definition of, 82
  examples of, 82–85

frequency, law of, 87, 88
Freud, S., 28, 33, 34, 39, 41, 43, 55, 69, 72, 82
From the Workshop of Discoveries, 80
Furst, Bruno, 64

General and Social Psychology, 69
generalisation, principle of, 89
Gilliland, A. R., 26
Goethe, 35
Guides to Straight Thinking, 69

habit, 48
habit memory, 16, 102
hallucination, 18
Hood, Thomas, 30

imagination, 13, 102
immediate memory, 17
impression, 45–58
    weak, 24–25, 33, 97
inhibition, proactive, 27, 98–100, 104
    retroactive, 27, 98–100, 103
Inner Experience of a Psycho-Analyst, The, 83
inspiration, 80
intensity, law of, 87
intention to remember, 57
interest, 50–53
interference, 23, 27, 98–100, 103–104
    avoiding, 75–78, 106
Introductory Lectures on Psycho-Analysis, 82

Jacobsen, E., 54
James, William, 13, 49
Jenkins, J. G., 76
Johnson, 76

Korsakoff syndrome, 39

language study, 68–69, 91
law of reversed effort, 78
Lewin, Kurt, 70

Life Triumphant, 96
"little and often," 61–63, 105
Loewi, O., 80
logical memory, 17

meaning, memory and, 59–61
memorising, 21
memory for completed and un-completed tasks, 69–72, 106
memory images, types of, 18
memory, is it a "faculty"?, 14
memory optimists, 30–32
    pessimists, 30–32
memory span, 17
memory trace, 13, 23, 25, 27, 75, 97, 102
    energy of, 23
memory, types of, 16
memory, what is it?, 13–22, 102
Miller, Henry Knight, 24, 60, 96, 97, 98
Morse code, 66
motiles, 19
Muensterberg, 54

names, remembering, 65

olfactory memory, 20
"one-word" translation, 90
overlearning, 59, 64–66, 105

phonetic alphabet, 63
Practical Psychology, 24, 60
"practice makes perfect," 88
predominant mental impression, law of, 24
proactive inhibition, 27, 98–100, 104
problems solved in sleep, 80
Progressive Relaxation, 54
pure memory, 16, 102

recalling, 21
recall, methods of, 78–85
recency, law of, 31, 87
recitation, 59, 63–64, 105
    reasons for, 63

Reik, T., 83
reincarnation, 41
Reincarnation for Everyman, 41
reintegration, 59, 68–69, 81, 105
  examples of, 81–82
relaxation, 53–55
remember, how to, 45–95, 105–107
  intention to, 57
remembering, definition of, 13, 102
  summary of practical hints on,
    102–107
  the English counties, 92
  theories of, 13
  ways of, 21
remote memory, 17
repetition, 58–75, 105
  experimental proof of value of,
    58
  conditions under which effective,
    59–75, 105–106
repression, 24, 27, 33, 72, 78–80,
    100, 104, 106, 108
  and maladjustment, 30
  definition of, 27–28
  experimental proofs of, 29–30
  methods of relieving, 78–85, 106
  reasons for, 28–29
retention, 21
retroactive inhibition, 27, 98–100,
    103
*Right Way to Interpret Your
  Dreams, The*, 79
Roback, A. A., 16
Robinson, E. S., 42
Rosenzweig, S., 71
rote memory, 17

screen memories, 34
scriptural texts, memorising, 67
Seibert, L. C., 66
similarity, 86, 98, 103
skill, acquiring, 62
"sleeping on it," 80, 107
spaced learning, 59, 61–63
speech, how to remember, 93–94
style of life, 35–38
Swan, 76

tactiles, 20
task-orientation, 72
Taylor, C., 30
tension, 53–55
"thingummybob" principle, 13
thinking, 13, 102
Thompson, G. G., 32
Thorndike, 60, 88
Thouless, R. H., 54, 69

visiles, 19
vividness, law of, 87, 99
von Restorff effect, 72

Watkins, D. E., 94
whole learning, 59, 66–67, 105
Witryol, S. L., 32
worry, 55–57

Zeigarnik effect, 59, 69–72, 106
  illustrations of, 70–72
  reversal of, 71, 106
Zeller, A. F., 30

A Personal Word From Melvin Powers
Publisher, Wilshire Book Company

Dear Friend:

My goal is to publish interesting, informative, and inspirational books. You can help me accomplish this by answering the following questions, either by phone or by mail. Or, if convenient for you, I would welcome the opportunity to visit with you in my office and hear your comments in person.

Did you enjoy reading this book? Why?

Would you enjoy reading another similar book?

What idea in the book impressed you the most?

If applicable to your situation, have you incorporated this idea in your daily life?

Is there a chapter that could serve as a theme for an entire book? Please explain.

If you have an idea for a book, I would welcome discussing it with you. If you already have one in progress, write or call me concerning possible publication. I can be reached at (213) 875-1711 or (213) 983-1105.

Sincerely yours,

Melvin Powers

12015 Sherman Road
North Hollywood, California 91605

MELVIN POWERS SELF-IMPROVEMENT LIBRARY

ASTROLOGY

_____ASTROLOGY: HOW TO CHART YOUR HOROSCOPE _Max Heindel_ 3.00
_____ASTROLOGY: YOUR PERSONAL SUN-SIGN GUIDE _Beatrice Ryder_ 3.00
_____ASTROLOGY FOR EVERYDAY LIVING _Janet Harris_ 2.00
_____ASTROLOGY MADE EASY _Astarte_ 3.00
_____ASTROLOGY MADE PRACTICAL _Alexandra Kayhle_ 3.00
_____ASTROLOGY, ROMANCE, YOU AND THE STARS _Anthony Norvell_ 4.00
_____MY WORLD OF ASTROLOGY _Sydney Omarr_ 5.00
_____THOUGHT DIAL _Sydney Omarr_ 4.00
_____WHAT THE STARS REVEAL ABOUT THE MEN IN YOUR LIFE _Thelma White_ 3.00

BRIDGE

_____BRIDGE BIDDING MADE EASY _Edwin B. Kantar_ 7.00
_____BRIDGE CONVENTIONS _Edwin B. Kantar_ 5.00
_____BRIDGE HUMOR _Edwin B. Kantar_ 5.00
_____COMPETITIVE BIDDING IN MODERN BRIDGE _Edgar Kaplan_ 4.00
_____DEFENSIVE BRIDGE PLAY COMPLETE _Edwin B. Kantar_ 10.00
_____GAMESMAN BRIDGE—Play Better with Kantar _Edwin B. Kantar_ 5.00
_____HOW TO IMPROVE YOUR BRIDGE _Alfred Sheinwold_ 3.00
_____IMPROVING YOUR BIDDING SKILLS _Edwin B. Kantar_ 4.00
_____INTRODUCTION TO DEFENDER'S PLAY _Edwin B. Kantar_ 3.00
_____SHORT CUT TO WINNING BRIDGE _Alfred Sheinwold_ 3.00
_____TEST YOUR BRIDGE PLAY _Edwin B. Kantar_ 3.00
_____VOLUME 2—TEST YOUR BRIDGE PLAY _Edwin B. Kantar_ 5.00
_____WINNING DECLARER PLAY _Dorothy Hayden Truscott_ 4.00

BUSINESS, STUDY & REFERENCE

_____CONVERSATION MADE EASY _Elliot Russell_ 3.00
_____EXAM SECRET _Dennis B. Jackson_ 3.00
_____FIX-IT BOOK _Arthur Symons_ 2.00
_____HOW TO DEVELOP A BETTER SPEAKING VOICE _M. Hellier_ 3.00
_____HOW TO MAKE A FORTUNE IN REAL ESTATE _Albert Winnikoff_ 4.00
_____INCREASE YOUR LEARNING POWER _Geoffrey A. Dudley_ 3.00
_____MAGIC OF NUMBERS _Robert Tocquet_ 2.00
_____PRACTICAL GUIDE TO BETTER CONCENTRATION _Melvin Powers_ 3.00
_____PRACTICAL GUIDE TO PUBLIC SPEAKING _Maurice Forley_ 3.00
_____7 DAYS TO FASTER READING _William S. Schaill_ 3.00
_____SONGWRITERS RHYMING DICTIONARY _Jane Shaw Whitfield_ 5.00
_____SPELLING MADE EASY _Lester D. Basch & Dr. Milton Finkelstein_ 2.00
_____STUDENT'S GUIDE TO BETTER GRADES _J. A. Rickard_ 3.00
_____TEST YOURSELF—Find Your Hidden Talent _Jack Shafer_ 3.00
_____YOUR WILL & WHAT TO DO ABOUT IT _Attorney Samuel G. Kling_ 3.00

CALLIGRAPHY

_____ADVANCED CALLIGRAPHY _Katherine Jeffares_ 7.00
_____CALLIGRAPHER'S REFERENCE BOOK _Anne Leptich & Jacque Evans_ 6.00
_____CALLIGRAPHY—The Art of Beautiful Writing _Katherine Jeffares_ 7.00
_____CALLIGRAPHY FOR FUN & PROFIT _Anne Leptich & Jacque Evans_ 7.00
_____CALLIGRAPHY MADE EASY _Tina Serafini_ 7.00

CHESS & CHECKERS

_____BEGINNER'S GUIDE TO WINNING CHESS _Fred Reinfeld_ 3.00
_____CHECKERS MADE EASY _Tom Wiswell_ 2.00
_____CHESS IN TEN EASY LESSONS _Larry Evans_ 3.00
_____CHESS MADE EASY _Milton L. Hanauer_ 3.00
_____CHESS PROBLEMS FOR BEGINNERS _edited by Fred Reinfeld_ 2.00
_____CHESS SECRETS REVEALED _Fred Reinfeld_ 2.00
_____CHESS STRATEGY—An Expert's Guide _Fred Reinfeld_ 2.00
_____CHESS TACTICS FOR BEGINNERS _edited by Fred Reinfeld_ 3.00
_____CHESS THEORY & PRACTICE _Morry & Mitchell_ 2.00
_____HOW TO WIN AT CHECKERS _Fred Reinfeld_ 3.00
_____1001 BRILLIANT WAYS TO CHECKMATE _Fred Reinfeld_ 4.00
_____1001 WINNING CHESS SACRIFICES & COMBINATIONS _Fred Reinfeld_ 4.00
_____SOVIET CHESS _Edited by R. G. Wade_ 3.00

COOKERY & HERBS

CULPEPER'S HERBAL REMEDIES *Dr. Nicholas Culpeper* — 3.00
FAST GOURMET COOKBOOK *Poppy Cannon* — 2.50
GINSENG The Myth & The Truth *Joseph P. Hou* — 3.00
HEALING POWER OF HERBS *May Bethel* — 3.00
HEALING POWER OF NATURAL FOODS *May Bethel* — 3.00
HERB HANDBOOK *Dawn MacLeod* — 3.00
HERBS FOR COOKING AND HEALING *Dr. Donald Law* — 2.00
HERBS FOR HEALTH—How to Grow & Use Them *Louise Evans Doole* — 3.00
HOME GARDEN COOKBOOK—Delicious Natural Food Recipes *Ken Kraft* — 3.00
MEDICAL HERBALIST *edited by Dr. J. R. Yemm* — 3.00
NATURAL FOOD COOKBOOK *Dr. Harry C. Bond* — 3.00
NATURE'S MEDICINES *Richard Lucas* — 3.00
VEGETABLE GARDENING FOR BEGINNERS *Hugh Wiberg* — 2.00
VEGETABLES FOR TODAY'S GARDENS *R. Milton Carleton* — 2.00
VEGETARIAN COOKERY *Janet Walker* — 4.00
VEGETARIAN COOKING MADE EASY & DELECTABLE *Veronica Vezza* — 3.00
VEGETARIAN DELIGHTS—A Happy Cookbook for Health *K. R. Mehta* — 2.00
VEGETARIAN GOURMET COOKBOOK *Joyce McKinnel* — 3.00

GAMBLING & POKER

ADVANCED POKER STRATEGY & WINNING PLAY *A. D. Livingston* — 3.00
HOW NOT TO LOSE AT POKER *Jeffrey Lloyd Castle* — 3.00
HOW TO WIN AT DICE GAMES *Skip Frey* — 3.00
HOW TO WIN AT POKER *Terence Reese & Anthony T. Watkins* — 3.00
SECRETS OF WINNING POKER *George S. Coffin* — 3.00
WINNING AT CRAPS *Dr. Lloyd T. Commins* — 3.00
WINNING AT GIN *Chester Wander & Cy Rice* — 3.00
WINNING AT POKER—An Expert's Guide *John Archer* — 3.00
WINNING AT 21—An Expert's Guide *John Archer* — 4.00
WINNING POKER SYSTEMS *Norman Zadeh* — 3.00

HEALTH

BEE POLLEN *Lynda Lyngheim & Jack Scagnetti* — 3.00
DR. LINDNER'S SPECIAL WEIGHT CONTROL METHOD *P. G. Lindner, M.D.* — 1.50
HELP YOURSELF TO BETTER SIGHT *Margaret Darst Corbett* — 3.00
HOW TO IMPROVE YOUR VISION *Dr. Robert A. Kraskin* — 3.00
HOW YOU CAN STOP SMOKING PERMANENTLY *Ernest Caldwell* — 3.00
MIND OVER PLATTER *Peter G. Lindner, M.D.* — 3.00
NATURE'S WAY TO NUTRITION & VIBRANT HEALTH *Robert J. Scrutton* — 3.00
NEW CARBOHYDRATE DIET COUNTER *Patti Lopez-Pereira* — 1.50
QUICK & EASY EXERCISES FOR FACIAL BEAUTY *Judy Smith-deal* — 2.00
QUICK & EASY EXERCISES FOR FIGURE BEAUTY *Judy Smith-deal* — 2.00
REFLEXOLOGY *Dr. Maybelle Segal* — 3.00
REFLEXOLOGY FOR GOOD HEALTH *Anna Kaye & Don C. Matchan* — 3.00
YOU CAN LEARN TO RELAX *Dr. Samuel Gutwirth* — 3.00
YOUR ALLERGY—What To Do About It *Allan Knight, M.D.* — 3.00

HOBBIES

BEACHCOMBING FOR BEGINNERS *Norman Hickin* — 2.00
BLACKSTONE'S MODERN CARD TRICKS *Harry Blackstone* — 3.00
BLACKSTONE'S SECRETS OF MAGIC *Harry Blackstone* — 3.00
COIN COLLECTING FOR BEGINNERS *Burton Hobson & Fred Reinfeld* — 3.00
ENTERTAINING WITH ESP *Tony 'Doc' Shiels* — 2.00
400 FASCINATING MAGIC TRICKS YOU CAN DO *Howard Thurston* — 3.00
HOW I TURN JUNK INTO FUN AND PROFIT *Sari* — 3.00
HOW TO WRITE A HIT SONG & SELL IT *Tommy Boyce* — 7.00
JUGGLING MADE EASY *Rudolf Dittrich* — 2.00
MAGIC FOR ALL AGES *Walter Gibson* — 4.00
MAGIC MADE EASY *Byron Wels* — 2.00
STAMP COLLECTING FOR BEGINNERS *Burton Hobson* — 2.00

HORSE PLAYERS' WINNING GUIDES

BETTING HORSES TO WIN *Les Conklin* — 3.00
ELIMINATE THE LOSERS *Bob McKnight* — 3.00

_____HOW TO PICK WINNING HORSES _Bob McKnight_	3.00
_____HOW TO WIN AT THE RACES _Sam (The Genius) Lewin_	3.00
_____HOW YOU CAN BEAT THE RACES _Jack Kavanagh_	3.00
_____MAKING MONEY AT THE RACES _David Barr_	3.00
_____PAYDAY AT THE RACES _Les Conklin_	3.00
_____SMART HANDICAPPING MADE EASY _William Bauman_	3.00
_____SUCCESS AT THE HARNESS RACES _Barry Meadow_	3.00
_____WINNING AT THE HARNESS RACES—An Expert's Guide _Nick Cammarano_	3.00

HUMOR

_____HOW TO BE A COMEDIAN FOR FUN & PROFIT _King & Laufer_	2.00
_____HOW TO FLATTEN YOUR TUSH _Coach Marge Reardon_	2.00
_____JOKE TELLER'S HANDBOOK _Bob Orben_	3.00
_____JOKES FOR ALL OCCASIONS _Al Schock_	3.00
_____2000 NEW LAUGHS FOR SPEAKERS _Bob Orben_	3.00
_____2,500 JOKES TO START 'EM LAUGHING _Bob Orben_	3.00

HYPNOTISM

_____ADVANCED TECHNIQUES OF HYPNOSIS _Melvin Powers_	2.00
_____BRAINWASHING AND THE CULTS _Paul A. Verdier, Ph.D._	3.00
_____CHILDBIRTH WITH HYPNOSIS _William S. Kroger, M.D._	3.00
_____HOW TO SOLVE Your Sex Problems with Self-Hypnosis _Frank S. Caprio, M.D._	3.00
_____HOW TO STOP SMOKING THRU SELF-HYPNOSIS _Leslie M. LeCron_	3.00
_____HOW TO USE AUTO-SUGGESTION EFFECTIVELY _John Duckworth_	3.00
_____HOW YOU CAN BOWL BETTER USING SELF-HYPNOSIS _Jack Heise_	3.00
_____HOW YOU CAN PLAY BETTER GOLF USING SELF-HYPNOSIS _Jack Heise_	3.00
_____HYPNOSIS AND SELF-HYPNOSIS _Bernard Hollander, M.D._	3.00
_____HYPNOTISM _(Originally published in 1893) Carl Sextus_	5.00
_____HYPNOTISM & PSYCHIC PHENOMENA _Simeon Edmunds_	4.00
_____HYPNOTISM MADE EASY _Dr. Ralph Winn_	3.00
_____HYPNOTISM MADE PRACTICAL _Louis Orton_	3.00
_____HYPNOTISM REVEALED _Melvin Powers_	2.00
_____HYPNOTISM TODAY _Leslie LeCron and Jean Bordeaux, Ph.D._	5.00
_____MODERN HYPNOSIS _Lesley Kuhn & Salvatore Russo, Ph.D._	5.00
_____NEW CONCEPTS OF HYPNOSIS _Bernard C. Gindes, M.D._	5.00
_____NEW SELF-HYPNOSIS _Paul Adams_	4.00
_____POST-HYPNOTIC INSTRUCTIONS—Suggestions for Therapy _Arnold Furst_	3.00
_____PRACTICAL GUIDE TO SELF-HYPNOSIS _Melvin Powers_	3.00
_____PRACTICAL HYPNOTISM _Philip Magonet, M.D._	3.00
_____SECRETS OF HYPNOTISM _S. J. Van Pelt, M.D._	3.00
_____SELF-HYPNOSIS A Conditioned-Response Technique _Laurance Sparks_	5.00
_____SELF-HYPNOSIS Its Theory, Technique & Application _Melvin Powers_	3.00
_____THERAPY THROUGH HYPNOSIS _edited by Raphael H. Rhodes_	4.00

JUDAICA

_____HOW TO LIVE A RICHER & FULLER LIFE _Rabbi Edgar F. Magnin_	2.00
_____MODERN ISRAEL _Lily Edelman_	2.00
_____SERVICE OF THE HEART _Evelyn Garfiel, Ph.D._	4.00
_____STORY OF ISRAEL IN COINS _Jean & Maurice Gould_	2.00
_____STORY OF ISRAEL IN STAMPS _Maxim & Gabriel Shamir_	1.00
_____TONGUE OF THE PROPHETS _Robert St.John_	5.00

JUST FOR WOMEN

_____COSMOPOLITAN'S GUIDE TO MARVELOUS MEN Fwd. by _Helen Gurley Brown_	3.00
_____COSMOPOLITAN'S HANG-UP HANDBOOK Foreword by _Helen Gurley Brown_	4.00
_____COSMOPOLITAN'S LOVE BOOK—A Guide to Ecstasy in Bed	4.00
_____COSMOPOLITAN'S NEW ETIQUETTE GUIDE Fwd. by _Helen Gurley Brown_	4.00
_____I AM A COMPLEAT WOMAN _Doris Hagopian & Karen O'Connor Sweeney_	3.00
_____JUST FOR WOMEN—A Guide to the Female Body _Richard E. Sand, M.D._	4.00
_____NEW APPROACHES TO SEX IN MARRIAGE _John E. Eichenlaub, M.D._	3.00
_____SEXUALLY ADEQUATE FEMALE _Frank S. Caprio, M.D._	3.00
_____YOUR FIRST YEAR OF MARRIAGE _Dr. Tom McGinnis_	3.00

MARRIAGE, SEX & PARENTHOOD

_____ABILITY TO LOVE _Dr. Allan Fromme_	5.00
_____ENCYCLOPEDIA OF MODERN SEX & LOVE TECHNIQUES _Macandrew_	5.00
_____GUIDE TO SUCCESSFUL MARRIAGE _Drs. Albert Ellis & Robert Harper_	5.00

_____HOW TO RAISE AN EMOTIONALLY HEALTHY, HAPPY CHILD *A. Ellis*   3.00

_____IMPOTENCE & FRIGIDITY *Edwin W. Hirsch, M.D.*   3.00

_____SEX WITHOUT GUILT *Albert Ellis, Ph.D.*   3.00

_____SEXUALLY ADEQUATE MALE *Frank S. Caprio, M.D.*   3.00

MELVIN POWERS' MAIL ORDER LIBRARY

_____HOW TO GET RICH IN MAIL ORDER *Melvin Powers*   10.00

_____HOW TO WRITE A GOOD ADVERTISEMENT *Victor O. Schwab*   15.00

_____WORLD WIDE MAIL ORDER SHOPPER'S GUIDE *Eugene V. Moller*   5.00

METAPHYSICS & OCCULT

_____BOOK OF TALISMANS, AMULETS & ZODIACAL GEMS *William Pavitt*   4.00

_____CONCENTRATION—A Guide to Mental Mastery *Mouni Sadhu*   3.00

_____CRITIQUES OF GOD *Edited by Peter Angeles*   7.00

_____DREAMS & OMENS REVEALED *Fred Gettings*   3.00

_____EXTRA-TERRESTRIAL INTELLIGENCE—The First Encounter   6.00

_____FORTUNE TELLING WITH CARDS *P. Foli*   3.00

_____HANDWRITING ANALYSIS MADE EASY *John Marley*   3.00

_____HANDWRITING TELLS *Nadya Olyanova*   5.00

_____HOW TO UNDERSTAND YOUR DREAMS *Geoffrey A. Dudley*   3.00

_____ILLUSTRATED YOGA *William Zorn*   3.00

_____IN DAYS OF GREAT PEACE *Mouni Sadhu*   3.00

_____KING SOLOMON'S TEMPLE IN THE MASONIC TRADITION *Alex Horne*   5.00

_____LSD—THE AGE OF MIND *Bernard Roseman*   2.00

_____MAGICIAN—His training and work *W. E. Butler*   3.00

_____MEDITATION *Mouni Sadhu*   5.00

_____MODERN NUMEROLOGY *Morris C. Goodman*   3.00

_____NUMEROLOGY—ITS FACTS AND SECRETS *Ariel Yvon Taylor*   3.00

_____NUMEROLOGY MADE EASY *W. Mykian*   3.00

_____PALMISTRY MADE EASY *Fred Gettings*   3.00

_____PALMISTRY MADE PRACTICAL *Elizabeth Daniels Squire*   3.00

_____PALMISTRY SECRETS REVEALED *Henry Frith*   3.00

_____PROPHECY IN OUR TIME *Martin Ebon*   2.50

_____PSYCHOLOGY OF HANDWRITING *Nadya Olyanova*   3.00

_____SUPERSTITION—Are you superstitious? *Eric Maple*   2.00

_____TAROT *Mouni Sadhu*   6.00

_____TAROT OF THE BOHEMIANS *Papus*   5.00

_____WAYS TO SELF-REALIZATION *Mouni Sadhu*   3.00

_____WHAT YOUR HANDWRITING REVEALS *Albert E. Hughes*   2.00

_____WITCHCRAFT, MAGIC & OCCULTISM—A Fascinating History *W. B. Crow*   5.00

_____WITCHCRAFT—THE SIXTH SENSE *Justine Glass*   4.00

_____WORLD OF PSYCHIC RESEARCH *Hereward Carrington*   2.00

SELF-HELP & INSPIRATIONAL

_____DAILY POWER FOR JOYFUL LIVING *Dr. Donald Curtis*   3.00

_____DYNAMIC THINKING *Melvin Powers*   2.00

_____EXUBERANCE—Your Guide to Happiness & Fulfillment *Dr. Paul Kurtz*   3.00

_____GREATEST POWER IN THE UNIVERSE *U. S. Andersen*   5.00

_____GROW RICH WHILE YOU SLEEP *Ben Sweetland*   3.00

_____GROWTH THROUGH REASON *Albert Ellis, Ph.D.*   4.00

_____GUIDE TO DEVELOPING YOUR POTENTIAL *Herbert A. Otto, Ph.D.*   3.00

_____GUIDE TO LIVING IN BALANCE *Frank S. Caprio, M.D.*   2.00

_____HELPING YOURSELF WITH APPLIED PSYCHOLOGY *R. Henderson*   2.00

_____HELPING YOURSELF WITH PSYCHIATRY *Frank S. Caprio, M.D.*   2.00

_____HOW TO ATTRACT GOOD LUCK *A. H. Z. Carr*   4.00

_____HOW TO CONTROL YOUR DESTINY *Norvell*   3.00

_____HOW TO DEVELOP A WINNING PERSONALITY *Martin Panzer*   3.00

_____HOW TO DEVELOP AN EXCEPTIONAL MEMORY *Young & Gibson*   4.00

_____HOW TO OVERCOME YOUR FEARS *M. P. Leahy, M.D.*   3.00

_____HOW YOU CAN HAVE CONFIDENCE AND POWER *Les Giblin*   3.00

_____HUMAN PROBLEMS & HOW TO SOLVE THEM *Dr. Donald Curtis*   4.00

_____I CAN *Ben Sweetland*   4.00

_____I WILL *Ben Sweetland*   3.00

_____LEFT-HANDED PEOPLE *Michael Barsley*   4.00

____MAGIC IN YOUR MIND *U. S. Andersen*		5.00
____MAGIC OF THINKING BIG *Dr. David J. Schwartz*		3.00
____MAGIC POWER OF YOUR MIND *Walter M. Germain*		4.00
____MENTAL POWER THROUGH SLEEP SUGGESTION *Melvin Powers*		3.00
____NEW GUIDE TO RATIONAL LIVING *Albert Ellis, Ph.D. & R. Harper, Ph.D.*		3.00
____OUR TROUBLED SELVES *Dr. Allan Fromme*		3.00
____PSYCHO-CYBERNETICS *Maxwell Maltz, M.D.*		2.00
____SCIENCE OF MIND IN DAILY LIVING *Dr. Donald Curtis*		3.00
____SECRET OF SECRETS *U. S. Andersen*		5.00
____SECRET POWER OF THE PYRAMIDS *U. S. Andersen*		5.00
____STUTTERING AND WHAT YOU CAN DO ABOUT IT *W. Johnson, Ph.D.*		2.50
____SUCCESS-CYBERNETICS *U. S. Andersen*		4.00
____10 DAYS TO A GREAT NEW LIFE *William E. Edwards*		3.00
____THINK AND GROW RICH *Napoleon Hill*		3.00
____THREE MAGIC WORDS *U. S. Andersen*		5.00
____TREASURY OF COMFORT *edited by Rabbi Sidney Greenberg*		5.00
____TREASURY OF THE ART OF LIVING *Sidney S. Greenberg*		5.00
____YOU ARE NOT THE TARGET *Laura Huxley*		4.00
____YOUR SUBCONSCIOUS POWER *Charles M. Simmons*		4.00
____YOUR THOUGHTS CAN CHANGE YOUR LIFE *Dr. Donald Curtis*		4.00

SPORTS

____BICYCLING FOR FUN AND GOOD HEALTH *Kenneth E. Luther*		2.00
____BILLIARDS—Pocket • Carom • Three Cushion *Clive Cottingham, Jr.*		3.00
____CAMPING-OUT 101 Ideas & Activities *Bruno Knobel*		2.00
____COMPLETE GUIDE TO FISHING *Vlad Evanoff*		2.00
____HOW TO IMPROVE YOUR RACQUETBALL *Lubarsky, Kaufman, & Scagnetti*		3.00
____HOW TO WIN AT POCKET BILLIARDS *Edward D. Knuchell*		4.00
____JOY OF WALKING *Jack Scagnetti*		3.00
____LEARNING & TEACHING SOCCER SKILLS *Eric Worthington*		3.00
____MOTORCYCLING FOR BEGINNERS *I. G. Edmonds*		3.00
____RACQUETBALL FOR WOMEN *Toni Hudson, Jack Scagnetti & Vince Rondone*		3.00
____RACQUETBALL MADE EASY *Steve Lubarsky, Rod Delson & Jack Scagnetti*		3.00
____SECRET OF BOWLING STRIKES *Dawson Taylor*		3.00
____SECRET OF PERFECT PUTTING *Horton Smith & Dawson Taylor*		3.00
____SOCCER—The game & how to play it *Gary Rosenthal*		3.00
____STARTING SOCCER *Edward F. Dolan, Jr.*		3.00
____TABLE TENNIS MADE EASY *Johnny Leach*		2.00

TENNIS LOVERS' LIBRARY

____BEGINNER'S GUIDE TO WINNING TENNIS *Helen Hull Jacobs*		2.00
____HOW TO BEAT BETTER TENNIS PLAYERS *Loring Fiske*		4.00
____HOW TO IMPROVE YOUR TENNIS—Style, Strategy & Analysis *C. Wilson*		2.00
____INSIDE TENNIS—Techniques of Winning *Jim Leighton*		3.00
____PLAY TENNIS WITH ROSEWALL *Ken Rosewall*		2.00
____PSYCH YOURSELF TO BETTER TENNIS *Dr. Walter A. Luszki*		2.00
____SUCCESSFUL TENNIS *Neale Fraser*		2.00
____TENNIS FOR BEGINNERS *Dr. H. A. Murray*		2.00
____TENNIS MADE EASY *Joel Brecheen*		2.00
____WEEKEND TENNIS—How to have fun & win at the same time *Bill Talbert*		3.00
____WINNING WITH PERCENTAGE TENNIS—Smart Strategy *Jack Lowe*		2.00

WILSHIRE PET LIBRARY

____DOG OBEDIENCE TRAINING *Gust Kessopulos*		4.00
____DOG TRAINING MADE EASY & FUN *John W. Kellogg*		3.00
____HOW TO BRING UP YOUR PET DOG *Kurt Unkelbach*		2.00
____HOW TO RAISE & TRAIN YOUR PUPPY *Jeff Griffen*		2.00
____PIGEONS: HOW TO RAISE & TRAIN THEM *William H. Allen, Jr.*		2.00

*The books listed above can be obtained from your book dealer or directly from
Melvin Powers. When ordering, please remit 50¢ per book postage & handling.
Send for our free illustrated catalog of self-improvement books.*

Melvin Powers

12015 Sherman Road, No. Hollywood, California 91605

WILSHIRE HORSE LOVERS' LIBRARY

AMATEUR HORSE BREEDER *A. C. Leighton Hardman*	4.00
AMERICAN QUARTER HORSE IN PICTURES *Margaret Cabell Self*	3.00
APPALOOSA HORSE *Donna & Bill Richardson*	3.00
ARABIAN HORSE *Reginald S. Summerhays*	3.00
ART OF WESTERN RIDING *Suzanne Norton Jones*	3.00
AT THE HORSE SHOW *Margaret Cabell Self*	3.00
BACK-YARD FOAL *Peggy Jett Pittinger*	3.00
BACK-YARD HORSE *Peggy Jett Pittinger*	3.00
BASIC DRESSAGE *Jean Froissard*	2.00
BEGINNER'S GUIDE TO HORSEBACK RIDING *Sheila Wall*	2.00
BEGINNER'S GUIDE TO THE WESTERN HORSE *Natlee Kenoyer*	2.00
BITS—THEIR HISTORY, USE AND MISUSE *Louis Taylor*	3.00
BREAKING & TRAINING THE DRIVING HORSE *Doris Ganton*	3.00
BREAKING YOUR HORSE'S BAD HABITS *W. Dayton Sumner*	4.00
CAVALRY MANUAL OF HORSEMANSHIP *Gordon Wright*	3.00
COMPLETE TRAINING OF HORSE AND RIDER *Colonel Alois Podhajsky*	4.00
DISORDERS OF THE HORSE & WHAT TO DO ABOUT THEM *E. Hanauer*	3.00
DOG TRAINING MADE EASY & FUN *John W. Kellogg*	3.00
DRESSAGE—A Study of the Finer Points in Riding *Henry Wynmalen*	4.00
DRIVING HORSES *Sallie Walrond*	3.00
ENDURANCE RIDING *Ann Hyland*	2.00
EQUITATION *Jean Froissard*	4.00
FIRST AID FOR HORSES *Dr. Charles H. Denning, Jr.*	2.00
FUN OF RAISING A COLT *Rubye & Frank Griffith*	3.00
FUN ON HORSEBACK *Margaret Cabell Self*	4.00
GYMKHANA GAMES *Natlee Kenoyer*	2.00
HORSE DISEASES—Causes, Symptoms & Treatment *Dr. H. G. Belschner*	4.00
HORSE OWNER'S CONCISE GUIDE *Elsie V. Hanauer*	2.00
HORSE SELECTION & CARE FOR BEGINNERS *George H. Conn*	4.00
HORSEBACK RIDING FOR BEGINNERS *Louis Taylor*	4.00
HORSEBACK RIDING MADE EASY & FUN *Sue Henderson Coen*	4.00
HORSES—Their Selection, Care & Handling *Margaret Cabell Self*	3.00
HOW TO BUY A BETTER HORSE & SELL THE HORSE YOU OWN	3.00
HOW TO ENJOY YOUR QUARTER HORSE *Williard H. Porter*	3.00
HUNTER IN PICTURES *Margaret Cabell Self*	2.00
ILLUSTRATED BOOK OF THE HORSE *S. Sidney* (8½" x 11")	10.00
ILLUSTRATED HORSE MANAGEMENT—400 Illustrations *Dr. E. Mayhew*	6.00
ILLUSTRATED HORSE TRAINING *Captain M. H. Hayes*	5.00
ILLUSTRATED HORSEBACK RIDING FOR BEGINNERS *Jeanne Mellin*	3.00
JUMPING—Learning & Teaching *Jean Froissard*	4.00
KNOW ALL ABOUT HORSES *Harry Disston*	3.00
LAME HORSE—Causes, Symptoms & Treatment *Dr. James R. Rooney*	4.00
LAW & YOUR HORSE *Edward H. Greene*	5.00
LIPIZZANERS & THE SPANISH RIDING SCHOOL *W. Reuter* (4¼" x 6")	2.50
MANUAL OF HORSEMANSHIP *Harold Black*	5.00
MOVIE HORSES—The Fascinating Techniques of Training *Anthony Amaral*	2.00
POLICE HORSES *Judith Campbell*	2.00
PRACTICAL GUIDE TO HORSESHOEING	3.00
PRACTICAL GUIDE TO OWNING YOUR OWN HORSE *Steven D. Price*	3.00
PRACTICAL HORSE PSYCHOLOGY *Moyra Williams*	4.00
PROBLEM HORSES Guide for Curing Serious Behavior Habits *Summerhays*	3.00
REINSMAN OF THE WEST—BRIDLES & BITS *Ed Connell*	4.00
RESCHOOLING THE THOROUGHBRED *Peggy Jett Pittenger*	3.00
RIDE WESTERN *Louis Taylor*	3.00
SCHOOLING YOUR YOUNG HORSE *George Wheatley*	3.00
STABLE MANAGEMENT FOR THE OWNER-GROOM *George Wheatley*	4.00
STALLION MANAGEMENT—A Guide for Stud Owners *A. C. Hardman*	3.00
TEACHING YOUR HORSE TO JUMP *W. J. Froud*	2.00
TRAIL HORSES & TRAIL RIDING *Anne & Perry Westbrook*	2.00
TRAINING YOUR HORSE TO SHOW *Neale Haley*	4.00
TREATING COMMON DISEASES OF YOUR HORSE *Dr. George H. Conn*	3.00
TREATING HORSE AILMENTS *G. W. Serth*	2.00
YOU AND YOUR PONY *Pepper Mainwaring Healey* (8½" x 11")	6.00
YOUR FIRST HORSE *George C. Saunders, M.D.*	3.00
YOUR PONY BOOK *Hermann Wiederhold*	2.00

*The books listed above can be obtained from your book dealer or directly from
Melvin Powers. When ordering, please remit 50¢ per book postage & handling.
Send for our free illustrated catalog of self-improvement books.*

Melvin Powers
12015 Sherman Road, No. Hollywood, California 91605